Drew,

I hope you receive as much pleasure reading my book as I did in collecting everything in it

To [signature] To

THE WORLD OF TOMORROW

THE 1939 NEW YORK WORLD'S FAIR

Overleaf: Visible for miles around, a flood of multicolored light drenches the sky above the glowing spectacle which is the New York World's Fair at night. With the exception of the Persiphere, none of the buildings of the Fair were floodlighted, both the interior and exterior of most structures having been illumnated by built-in lighting that formed a part of the architectural design. Here capillary mercury tubes, illuminating masses of foliage from beneath, transform Constitution Mall into a glittering ribbon of silver and gold.

THE WORLD OF

LARRY ZIM   MEL LERNER   HERBERT ROLFES

TOMORROW

THE 1939 NEW YORK WORLD'S FAIR

A **MAIN STREET PRESS** BOOK

1817

HARPER & ROW, PUBLISHERS, New York
Cambridge, Philadelphia, San Francisco, London
Mexico City, São Paulo, Sydney

For Larry Zim and Mel Lerner
as inseparable in memory as the T. and P.

FIRST EDITION 1988

Library of Congress Catalog Card Number: 88-45075
ISBN 0-06-015923-5

Designed by Ronald R. Misiur

Chapter 2 of the present work is excerpted from "The Fair—The City," a special supplement to *The New York Times*, April 30, 1939, and is reprinted by permission. Copyright © 1939 by The New York Times Company.

Photographs by Melville David Weingarten © Catherine Yronwode.

88 89 90 91 92 10 9 8 7 6 5 4 3 2 1

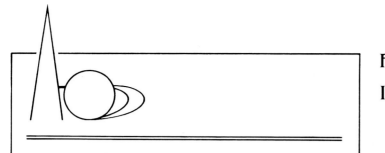

Contents

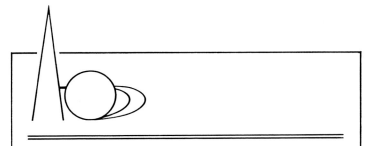

Foreword

For a fare of only five cents, fairgoers could take the I.R.T. and B.M.T. subways to the new World's Fair station at Willets Point, where an overpass led directly to the fairgrounds and onto Bowling Green Plaza. A subway ride from Times Square to the station took twenty-four minutes, and the terminal could handle 40,000 persons an hour. At Bowling Green the faint of foot could take special Greyhound buses (ten cents), tractor trains (twenty-five cents), or American Express "motoguide chairs" (one dollar for the first fifteen minutes) or single or double hand-pushed "guide chairs" (fifty and twenty-five cents respectively for the first fifteen minutes) to any point on the Fair's 1,216½ acres. At the center of Bowling Green was Waylande Gregory's "Fountain of the Atom."

How is one to regard the 1939 New York World's Fair, an event that simultaneously marked the end of one era and the beginning of another? "The persuasiveness of world's fairs is evident in their lasting effects upon history and our daily lives," writes Mitchell Wolfson, Jr. But Patricia Leigh Brown counters that "world's fairs, by their very nature, are ephemeral, freeze-frames in history that encapsulate the aspirations and values of a particular moment in time."

A half century after the Fair, its importance lies somewhere between Wolfson's "monumental beacon serving mankind" and Brown's fading snapshot. To Larry Zim, the purpose of a world's fair was to sell ideas and products; and the means, the architecture of fantasy. "World's fairs," he wrote, "are the show business of architecture. Mounted to dazzle and move large audiences, the architectural environments are both theater and performance." And, in saying this, he underscored what those who went to the fair in 1939 and 1940 remember most: it was dazzling, it was exciting, and it was fun.

In the summer of 1939, when he was eight years old, Larry Zim ran away from home—and, following the great form of the Trylon and Perisphere before him, made his way to the New York World's Fair. It was an experience that changed his life. His treasured "I Have Seen the Future" button and his green plastic Heinz pickle pin became the nucleus of what was to become one of the world's finest collections of exposition memorabilia.

With the zeal of a true believer tempered by an innate respect for the past, Larry Zim planned a golden anniversary commemorative volume that would capture the visual excitement that was the New York World's Fair. His plan was to take the reader on a tour of The World of Tomorrow, down the broad avenues radiating from the Trylon and Perisphere and into the streamlined pavilions that had fired his imagination when he was eight. But shortly after completing a first draft of the introduction, he died suddenly on April 7, 1987. The book was to have been completed by Mel Lerner, Larry's business partner and fellow designer whose knowledge of world's fairs was no less keen than his ability to appreciate them with a designer's eye, but not long after Larry's death, Mel Lerner died on January 7, 1988. In the wake of this terrible loss, Herbert Rolfes generously offered material from his own fine collection of world's fair memorabilia to make completion of this book possible.

The 1939 New York World's Fair is now a barely recoverable memory of what, despite the depressed thirties, was in fact an age of optimism. The present book, dedicated to Larry Zim and Mel Lerner, fulfills the goal of both: to recover that memory on the fiftieth anniversary of the event and to re-create in text and pictures the excitement and confidence in the future it generated.

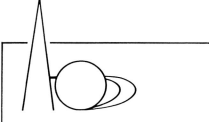

Introduction

President Franklin Delano Roosevelt, who officially opened the New York World's Fair with a brief dedicatory address, believed that "the only limit to our realization of tomorrow will be our doubts of today. Let us move forward," he exhorted, "with strong and active faith." Here, before the Trylon and Perisphere, indivisible emblems of all that was modern and forward-looking in 1939, two future citizens of the World of Tomorrow playfully embrace.

All who come to this World's Fair in New York . . . will receive the heartiest of welcomes. They will find that the eyes of the United States are fixed on the future. Our wagon is hitched to a star. But it is a star of good will, a star of progress for mankind, a star of greater happiness and less hardship, a star of international good will, and, above all, a star of peace. May the months to come carry us forward in the rays of that hope. I hereby dedicate the New York World's Fair of 1939 and declare it open to all mankind.

—From President Franklin Delano Roosevelt's address at the New York World's Fair opening ceremonies, April 30, 1939.

The idea of a world's fair in New York to celebrate the 150th anniversary of the inauguration of George Washington came first to Joseph F. Shadgen, a civil engineer who eventually sued the New York World's Fair Corporation for theft of his concept. Shadgen and Washington to the contrary, most people—even to this day—think of one man as synonymous with the fair, believing now as then that Grover Whalen, "official greeter" of New York City and a flamboyant man with a varied public and private career, originated the idea. To the businessmen who financed the fair and created the New York World's Fair Corporation to administer it, the inspiration was neither an occasion nor an anniversary, much less a patriotic impulse. Such things came later. The motive was business pure and simple, and the likely inspiration, the Chicago Century of Progress Exposition of 1933-34, financially successful against great odds in the worst years of the Depression. If the Second City could perform so admirably, what could prevent the success of an even more glorious event in an even greater city? The rationale for the fair eventually became Shadgen's celebration of Washington's inaugural; its secondary but best-remembered theme, "Building the World of Tomorrow," was an afterthought.

Neither democracy nor the world of tomorrow held much promise in 1939. Spain had had its terrible civil war, with a final victory for fascism. In March 1938, Germany annexed Austria, and in September 1938, Czechoslovakia. Italy had invaded Ethiopia three years earlier in October 1935. Japan and China were at war; a by-product of this war, which directly touched the United States as these other events did not, was the bombing of the gunboat *Panay* in December 1937. American opinion was divided: should Americans build up their armed forces, which were traditionally weak in peacetime, or should they avoid anything that looked like a preparation for getting involved? Fascism was by no means universally despised in the late 1930s in America, and involvement would imply fighting fascism, which was in the ascendant. All these matters had the United States jittery enough that the famous Orson Welles radio broadcast of October 30, 1938, convinced nearly two million people that Martians—or Nazis disguised as Martians—had invaded New Jersey, and this despite normal station breaks and a jocular goodbye from Welles himself on what was after all the day before Halloween. In September 1939, both Germany and Russia—temporary allies to the confounding of American communists—invaded Poland and quickly conquered it. Great Britain and France entered the battlefields that same month.

In the United States there was the slow recovery from the Depression, a recovery not completed in 1939, and trouble, sometimes violent, between organized labor and management. In their daily lives Americans generally were less interested in a distant future full of necessarily nebulous promise than in a proximate tomorrow with increased security and comfort.

The Depression, though, had had the effect of concentrating a considerable amount of talent on these very matters of security and comfort and, more than ever before, as they concerned the ordinary American. The socialists, the communists, and the technocrats offered political plans, much concerned with the economy, that promised to replace traditional capitalism—motivated as it was by a self-interest that often blundered—with something safer and more fair. Systems of flood control and rural electrification worked also toward security and comfort. The NRA and the WPA, with the other New Deal alphabet-soup agencies of government, tried to get laborers back to work at more or less meaningful jobs. Industrial design, a fledgling pre-Depression innovation, took what opportunities it could get to create neater, more efficient, and more aesthetically satisfying objects of use. Public housing, air conditioning, and radically new airliners helped various consumer classes to improve their lot in many ways. Two symbols of the 1930s might, indeed, be the streamlined automobile, a kind of utilitarian art form *for* the masses, and the post-office mural, painted by WPA artists and showing the life *of* the masses.

The 1939 New York World's Fair was held against a background of war that threatened to make its bright promises mere irony. And yet, to Americans still hoping against hope for neutrality, there was some meaning in the World of Tomorrow. Neither the celebrations of democracy nor what history was shown at the fair made a lasting impact, but the exalted materialism of the visionary commercial displays did.

What made these displays thrilling to the fairgoer of 1939 was a general credulousness, born of a belief in a beneficent technology, that has all but vanished in today's world. The average middle-aged fairgoer fifty years ago would have been a living witness to the greatest scientific advances in the history of the planet. Born into a world without automobiles, electric lights, airplanes, or telephones, he would have seen the rapid development, perfection, and dissemination of them all in slightly more than a single generation. Most people in 1939 were therefore dazzled by speed, by progress, by the new. The outlines of the fair were streamlined, futuristic, and intentionally original. It was a designer's fair from first to last.

For the site of the exposition, a fetid area three-and-a-half miles long, known locally as Corona Dumps, was leveled and filled to create the new Flushing Meadows Park. With good railroad, subway, highway, and water access from Manhattan, it was an obvious place to choose in a land-hungry urban complex. The idea of a theme suggested a Theme Center, and here a pair of the most famous world's fair structures, only less famous than the Crystal Palace of 1851 and the Eiffel Tower of 1889, were built: the Trylon, 700 feet high, and the Perisphere, 200 feet in diameter. From these, the zones of the exposition radiated, while Constitution Mall—named to commemorate the ratification of the United States Constitution in 1789—led past a gigantic statue of Washington to the stately pavilions beyond. Like several earlier fairs, the New York World's Fair was an encyclopedic exposition, with a plan that reflected the various subjects selected for exhibit, from transportation and community interests to production and communications. Three major divisions, which were in turn subdivided, occupied neat wedges of the plan with sixty-five buildings. Each division had its own distinctive color, echoed in the flower plantings, which deepened in hue the further the buildings got from the pure-white Theme Center until the outermost buildings were vividly red, gold, or blue. All these central buildings had to be original in design, imitating neither an existing building nor a historic style. The fair management built a "focal exhibit" for each subdivision, the other buildings being the work of the private exhibitors. Off to one side there was an amusement section, larger in area than the entire Paris Exposition of 1937 and built around an artificial lake. Elsewhere, thirty-three states and fifty-eight foreign countries—including Japan, Italy, and the Soviet Union, but *not* including Germany—built official pavilions to celebrate democracy as a way of government and as a way of life. Some of these countries were conquered before the fair closed for its first season in October 1939.

At Chicago's Century of Progress Exposition, for the first time in the history of modern fairs, lavish commercial displays threatened to steal the show from the official pavilions. At the New York fair, this threat became

Visitors to Democracity enter the Perisphere via the "longest moving stairway in the world," while others leave the enormous auditorium on the graceful Helicline.

a promise. Nothing could really upstage the Trylon and Perisphere, but two of the most memorable exhibits, one official in nature, one sponsored by a major corporation, came close. Both were industrial designers' utopias, looking forward to a future of peace and prosperity; both, being timed events and very well attended, could be reached only after a purgatorial waiting period on outside ramps.

The designer Henry Dreyfuss, in the Perisphere itself, presented Democracity, a six-minute automated performance given to spectators on two moving balconies that circled slowly around a city of tomorrow. After a narrated explanation of the city below, night fell, stars emerged, and ten simultaneous motion pictures showed marching workers converging on the central space. Orchestral and choral music reinforced the mood with increasing fervor, and the whole performance ended in a flash of light.

Sensational as this was, the Futurama, General Motors' celebration of the motorized, fully-employed America envisioned for 1960, was even more so. No theatrical production of the day could compete in drama with the spectacle that Norman Bel Geddes, assisted by

the architect Albert Kahn, provided. Once inside, the visitor descended a narrow ramp through a space where the road system of 1939, then that of 1960, outlined in lights and explained by a recorded voice, were displayed on a map of the United States. Pairs of moving chairs, mounted on a train of boothlike compartments, then took the visitor to a new space, where a model of a region as it might be in 1960 was spread before him. The effect was that of looking from the window of an airplane, and cunning variations of model scale made it look as if the plane was descending toward a city. Speakers in each compartment (which "blinkered" the visitor to concentrate his attention) explained what was passing by. Suddenly, the compartment swung away from the city, and behold, the visitor was actually at the street corner of the city, on a sidewalk system elevated above the traffic level, with bright new buildings around him. He got up, walked along the sidewalk, and eventually found his way out—but not before passing dozens of General Motors cars.

Both these exhibits—and the long lines that led to them—illustrate how display techniques at the 1939 fair were far in advance of anything that had been seen before. Recognizing that the American male is a technician at heart, General Motors had had an operating production line as the main feature of its 1933 exhibit in

A close-up view of the city of 1960, as predicted in General Motors' Futurama. Breathtaking architecture—with "each city block a complete unit in itself"— was to provide "space, sunshine, light, and air" for everyone, rich and poor alike.

Chicago. It was going to do the same for 1939 until Geddes, an industrial designer with extensive experience designing for the Broadway stage, persuaded the company to his more sweeping consumer-oriented vision, which treated the visitor as a being to be psychologically conditioned as much as informed.

Raymond Loewy, another pioneer industrial designer, was also in evidence at the fair, in the focal exhibit of the transportation section, which had films on the history of transportation as well as Loewy's own "rocketport of the future." The rockets, intended for intercontinental travel, were apparently to be shot from giant cannons. Better yet, there was "Railroads on Parade," a theatrical display of American trains, old and new, in action, and with the almost inevitable musical accompaniment—by Kurt Weill—scored for orchestra and chorus. Best of all in this exhibit was Loewy's latest streamlined locomotive, designed for the Pennsylvania Railroad and running effortlessly in place at sixty miles per hour.

The Westinghouse Corporation created a new twist in display technique by ostentatiously burying its chief exhibit—the Time Capsule, a seriously intended gift to future archaeologists that won the approval and participation of such scientists as Albert Einstein. Its documents, intended for recovery in A.D. 6939, were accompanied, unfortunately, by a message to the people of the future in a stilted prose style that was a period curiosity in itself.

It was such material things, so sensationally presented, that most people remembered. If they wore the "I Have Seen the Future" buttons that General Motors distributed (and would distribute again at the New York fair of 1964), it was the Geddes type of future, a future of objects and systems for making and organizing objects, that they had seen. In a way, the exposition as the modern world had known it since the Crystal Palace of 1851 died with the New York World's Fair of 1939—the old materialistic exposition that displayed the tools of civilization and took their wise use for granted. After World War II, the corporations still displayed lavishly, but the tone of the expositions—apart from the flashy and ill-remembered 1964 one—was more one of concern with life styles and, increasingly, with the problems and pleasures of the human condition. In 1939, the subtheme of Democracy was given poignant emphasis by the gathering clouds of war, but did not capture the American imagination in the way that the prophecies of material goods (and, by implication, the money to buy them) did. Perhaps the device on display that had the greatest effect on the consumer's future was the very early television set shown at the RCA pavilion (the image was only seven inches across), though it was only after the war that television began to become important, and several years later that both TV sets and programming achieved a kind of maturity.

Behind the scenes, of course, there were both triumphs and difficulties. The Bureau of International Exhibitions recognized the New York fair—it did not in the case of the concurrent Golden Gate International Exhibition in San Francisco—and foreign participation was initially excellent.* The city of New York prepared efficiently for an avalanche of visitors, and the rail service was exceptional, though a slower if more romantic

steamboat service failed. And yet attendance was not up to expectations, and Grover Whalen was detected in the act of passing employees through the turnstiles to inflate the gate. (Tourist business in Manhattan was also disappointing.) An expressly anti-Nazi Freedom Pavilion, a showplace for conquered peoples, was canceled because the promised site was withdrawn. And, despite much energy on everyone's part, some places, the amusement concessions especially, were not ready on opening day.

Nonetheless, the New York World's Fair is remembered as the standard by which other fairs are judged. This is partly because many Americans now alive saw this as their first exposition, but partly also because it really was a triumphant event, brilliantly conceived on a colossal scale, that occurred at a time when one great national trouble was ending and another had not quite begun.

---

* In 1928 a group of countries, seeking to supervise the holding of expositions so that harmful competition and other sources of trouble and annoyance could be eliminated, formed the Bureau of International Expositions. Member countries were voluntarily bound by B.I.E. rules, and expositions held in non-member countries therefore had to have its approval or risk meager participation. Grover Whalen attained the coveted approval, and good foreign participation, by promising—without authority to do so—that the United States was about to join. In fact, the United States finally joined more than two decades after Whalen's ruse.

OPENS
MAY 26
See
Hear
Play
Sándor
WORLD'S
FAIR
A CENTURY OF
PROGRESS
CHICAGO
1934

CHAPTER ONE

The Great Fairs of the Depression

In 1933 and 1934 Chicago was the site of the Century of Progress Exposition, commemorating the 100th anniversary of the city's founding and stressing progress in art, science, and industry during the preceding century. The exposition's extraordinary Art Deco buildings sounded a new note in daring architectural concepts and striking color contrasts. First exhibited at the fair was neon lighting which soon exerted its influence on practically every city in North America and Europe. This poster, created by the artist Sándor for the 1934 season, captures the dramatic modernism of the popular fair, the only exposition to make a profit during the Depression.

There had been fairs for centuries, and world's fairs since London's Great Exposition of 1851, but, neither before nor since, had there been the sheer number of large-scale commercial fairs that were held during the 1930s in Europe and America. These fairs, only highlights of which are illustrated in the pages that follow, had the effect of providing an antidote to the world's economic gloom. In a decade of terrible depression, fairs offered the illusion of better times, an escapism similar to, but more tangible than, Hollywood's palliatives. Exhibits recalling the heritage of the past and prophesying the world of tomorrow easily outdrew the reality of contemporary life.

But while the crowds that attended these fairs went to be amused and entertained, they were readily aware of the fairs' larger meaning, a meaning regularly voiced in newspaper and magazine accounts of the day: "If we could apply immediately all the scientific principles that are being demonstrated at the fair," wrote one visitor to Chicago's Century of Progress Exposition in 1933, "if we could put to work at full capacity all the instruments and machines that are shown, we should change almost overnight the life of man and the face of the earth."

The very architecture of most of these fairs was therefore provocatively utopian and appropriately experimental. As the architectural historian Arnold L. Lehman has observed, "the designers of the 1930s expositions—architects, landscape architects, interior designers, lighting engineers—used the psychological climate of the period to create their great white magical temporary cities that thrilled millions of awed visitors. And the illusions that were created seemed complete as the fairs nomadically left one environment only to be visually transported to another city, across a continent. For whatever the architectural differences, which were often decisively marked, the similar configurations of 1930s expositions was more pronounced. The materials and limitations of temporary construction often overwhelmed the differences of thematic gestures: of Chicago's stark modernism or Dallas's bold pre-Columbianism, of San Francisco's Pacifica motifs or New York's streamlined world of the future."

The expositions of the 1930s were thus a strange but often wonderful mixture of monumental structures and light and frivolous sculpture, murals, fountains, mechanisms, and entertainments—a melange of exuberant high spirits that makes much contemporary architecture formal and ponderous by comparison.

CHICAGO, 1933-1934

Unlike the Chicago World's Fair of 1893, which sought in its architecture and arrangement to recall the glory and grandeur of the past, the Century of Progress Exposition was planned to project the mind and imagination into the future. It was not to look back, but forward. It was to be a projection, not a recollection. It was to move the eye vertically, not horizontally. A Century of Progress was bathed in color by Joseph Urban, who used a palette of the highest intensity. Color served as decoration, helping to unify the vastly different building shapes and adding a distinctive theatrical quality. Despite widespread criticism of the fair's modernistic architecture, a style adapted to an American scale from the buildings of the 1925 Exposition Internationale in Paris, 38 million visitors to the reclaimed fairgrounds on the edge of Lake Michigan paid hard-earned Depression money to view such extraordinary structures as E. H. Bennett's and Arthur Brown, Jr.'s Federal Building (*right*) and Bennett's and Hubert Burnham's Travel and Transportation Building (*below*).

In 1933 the *Encyclopaedia Britannica* published in a limited edition a handsome large-format pictorial record of A Century of Progress. Included in the volume was a series of unsigned watercolor paintings of some of the most distinctive structures of the fair. Shown *clockwise from left* are renderings of the General Motors Building, the Federal Building, the Sky Ride, and the Hall of Science. (The Sky Ride advertised itself as "the supreme thrill of A Century of Progress." For forty cents—children, twenty-five cents—fairgoers ascended by elevator 625 feet to an observation tower for "an inspiring view you will remember all your life." For an additional forty cents, they descended to the 200-foot level where they entered a rocket car for a ride over the lagoon and the tops of the fair's tallest buildings.) The poster on the *opposite page*, featuring the Federal Building, was designed by Weimer Purcell for the Neely Printing Company.

Brussels, 1935
San Diego, 1935-1936
Dallas, 1936
Cleveland, 1937
Paris, 1937

With the exception of San Diego's International Exposition of 1935, whose buildings largely conformed to the Spanish Colonial Revival structures remaining in Balboa Park from the International Panama-California Exposition of 1915-1916, the buildings of these Depression-era fairs were strikingly modernistic. The Texas Centennial featured Art Deco buildings with a Mexican flavor and pulchritudinous guides known as "Rangerettes." The latter may have grown up to become the grandmothers of the Dallas Cowboys Cheerleaders, but the basic plan of the fair and many of the buildings have survived and are still in use as museums and exhibit halls.

Opposite page: Views of the modernistic exhibition hall at the Universal International Exposition, Brussels, Belgium, 1935, and postcards from the California-Pacific International Exposition, San Diego, California, 1935-36. (In the midst of conservative Spanish-Colonial buildings that dominated the exposition, the Ford Motor Company erected a circular glass structure that was pure Hollywood-1935 and the most popular exhibit at the fair.)

This page: A poster by Florian and a typical postcard from the Texas Centennial Exposition, Dallas, Texas, 1936. The fair commemorated the 100th anniversary of the founding of the Republic of Texas and was intended to pull the Lone Star State out of the Depression. (It didn't.) Also shown is a postcard from the Great Lakes Exposition, Cleveland, Ohio, 1937. The aurora borealis, simulated by lighting engineers, was also featured at the Texas Centennial.

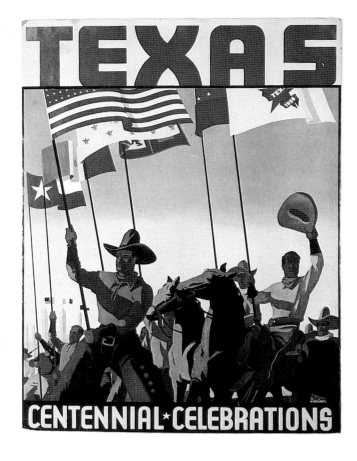

GL1 GROUNDS OF THE GREAT LAKES EXPOSITION AT NIGHT, LOOKING NORTH TOWARD LAKE ERIE,

SHOWING THE AURORA BOREALIS, CLEVELAND, OHIO

6A-H599

The Paris International Exposition of Art and Technology in Modern Life (1937) advanced the cause of modernism by showcasing, among others, the spectacular architecture of Alvar Aalto's Finnish Pavilion and the works of Joan Miró, Alexander Calder, and Pablo Picasso, whose haunting and powerfully political *Guernica* was first displayed there. The Eiffel Tower, covered in neon for the occasion, was flanked by the pavilions of Soviet Russia on the west and Nazi Germany on the east, ominously symbolic of the war soon to come. The poster on the *opposite page* is by Jean Carlu and was published by Bedos & Cie., Paris.

PAVILLON DE LA BELGIQUE
EXPO/ITION INTER ᴸᴱ
PARI/ ≈ 1937

That there was any fair at all in the Paris of 1937 was considered by most Europeans to be a miracle that only the French could have brought off. The political climate was oppressive: right was battling left; political riots were endemic; news of a German military build-up was alarming; the Spanish Civil War was too close for comfort; strikes delayed construction for months. When an unfinished fair opened in the spring of 1937, one visitor likened it to a disastrous dinner party where guests arrived to find the host tacking up silly decorations while the hostess argued with the kitchen staff. Still, the pavilions, best described as "conservative modern," were impressive and directly influenced American designers then planning buildings for the New York World's Fair.

SAN FRANCISCO, 1939

San Francisco's Golden Gate International Exposition opened on February 17, 1939, to commemorate the construction of the city's two new bridges, the Golden Gate Bridge and the Oakland Bay Bridge. An artificial island—created from once-dangerous shoals in San Francisco Bay and linked to the mainland by what was then the longest bridge in the world—was the site of the exposition and gave the fair the name by which it was popularly known, Treasure Island. Unlike the modernist buildings of the 1939 New York World's Fair, the exposition palaces on Treasure Island combined the beauty and drama of oriental and occidental architecture, marking the link between East and West that San Francisco considered itself to be. That the twain could indeed meet is illustrated by the coral-pink quasi-oriental Arch of Triumph (*above*), designed by Lewis P. Hobart, and the modern Federal Building, designed by Timothy L. Pflueger and featuring forty-eight columns, one for each state.

The Golden Gate Exposition billed itself as "A Pageant of the Pacific," but what this meant architecturally was the creation of a stucco South Seas fantasy that combined the modernism of Art Deco with the jungle daydreams of Depression Hollywood. The Court of the Moon and Stars (*right*), designed by George W. Kelham, had as its centerpiece "Evening Star," a sculpture by Ettore Cadorin. A pair of fanciful Elephant Towers (one seen in closeup *below*), designed by Donald Macky, flanked the main entrance to the fair. In the Court of Flowers (*below, right*), designed by Lewis P. Hobart, stood "Rainbow Girl," a sculptured fountain by O.C. Malmquist. The official fair poster by Vanderlaan (*opposite*), epitomized the exposition's "Pacific Basin" style.

CHAPTER TWO

The New York World's Fair Sees Itself

Sunday at the Fair. "To a visitor letting himself go with the crowd," wrote one observer, "we seem to be a race moving buoyantly toward a confident future, in a rhythm only partially broken by the ragtime of blistered and limping feet. No visitor who will let himself see truly what is before him will ever forget the Fair's emphasis on the conquest of natural forces, the fabulous might and delicacy of its machines, its underscoring of peace, plenty, and good will."

The following descriptive and statistical paragraphs, based on press releases from the New York World's Fair Corporation, appeared in a special World's Fair supplement to The New York Times *on opening day, Sunday, April 30, 1939:*

The biggest fair: The New York World's Fair is the biggest, the most costly fair ever held, offering the largest and most varied assortment of wonders and entertainments ever assembled under one sky.

With its 1,216 acres, it is three times the size of the current Golden Gate Fair, twice that of the Columbian Exposition of 1893. Its Amusement Zone alone would hold the entire Paris show of two years ago.

It has cost $155,000,000, as compared with 33 millions spent on Chicago's recent Century of Progress Exposition and 50 millions on the Panama-Pacific Fair of 1915.

It brings together sixty nations, most of the American states, and exhibitors by thousands from every craft and every land. At top speed it has an employed population of 50,000.

And it is going after the attendance record, with the grand total of 60,000,000 admissions in mind. The highest score it has to beat is that of the Century of Progress fair, which drew 39,000,000, but took two summers to do it.

The theme: It is a forward-looking fair. Its theme, the Future—"Building the World of Tomorrow with the Tools of Today." It takes just one backward glance; it celebrates the 150th anniversary of the inauguration, in this city, of George Washington as first President of the United States. Then it looks resolutely ahead and aims at recognizing the interdependence of men and nations, improving human welfare, bettering the American way of living and making this planet a happier one for all concerned.

It expresses the theme in its ground plan, its architecture, its use of color, its exhibits, all of them broadly hinting at what the world may be in years to come. It sums up the central idea in two white objects, immense and unique, visible for miles: the Perisphere, largest globe ever made by man, and the Trylon, a slender, three-sided spire 700 feet tall, one symbolizing the world about us, the other, aspiration.

Inside the Perisphere the Theme Exhibit sets the keynote for the Fair: "Democracity," a panoramic prophecy of the city of the future, a spectacle in which the dream of an ideal world takes form.

The layout: Viewed from the air, the Fair looks a bit like a many-colored fan spread over a space, one mile by three, containing three general areas, one for the main exhibits, one for government, one for amusements.

The Main Exhibit Area extends in all directions from the Perisphere and covers a mile square filled with buildings amazing in size, shape and hue, where architects, mural painters and landscape men have turned their imaginations loose. Here are found the Seven Focal Exhibits: Communications, Community Interests, Transportation, Medicine and Public Health, Science and Education, Food, and Production and Distribution, all conveniently arranged by kind in zones.

Beyond the Main Area to the east is the Government Area, a city of picturesque pavilions of foreign nations, centering on our own stately Federal Building. Away to the south of the Main Area for a mile or more stretches the Amusement Area beside its lake.

Eastward from the Theme Center runs the Main Street of the Fair and the middle rib of the fan, Constitution Mall, a broad avenue with pools, fountains, lawns, flower borders, shade trees and heroic statuary, including the eighty-five-foot figure of Washington and the sturdy "Four Freedoms" group. It ends at the Lagoon of Nations, where the crowds will gather nightly to witness the most gorgeous fireworks set off on earth since the Year One.

The exhibits: Here are the world's biggest locomotive, the world's smallest bonnet and almost everything in between. Virtually all the constructive activities of man are represented. The Fair brings the latest learning in countless fields and forecasts learning yet to come. It is strong for showing not things alone but also processes—how the things are made. It discloses what each individual owes to the work of other people, and vice versa. "We're all one family," says the Fair.

Each of the Focal Exhibits serves as a prologue to the drama of science, art, industry and accomplishment the Fair unfolds.

The amusements: Antarctic birds, amazons, midgets, showgirls, toboggan slides, parachute jumps, crazy dance floors, monkeys, mysterious caverns, live cobras, trips to the past and the future, electric shocks, electric eels, rocket rides, peep shows, Indians, shooting galleries, enchanted forests—why say more? Step up, step up, good people.

Place—time—price: The Fair occupies Flushing Meadows Park in the Borough of Queens, near the geographical heart of Greater New York City and within twenty minutes of midtown Manhattan. It can be reached

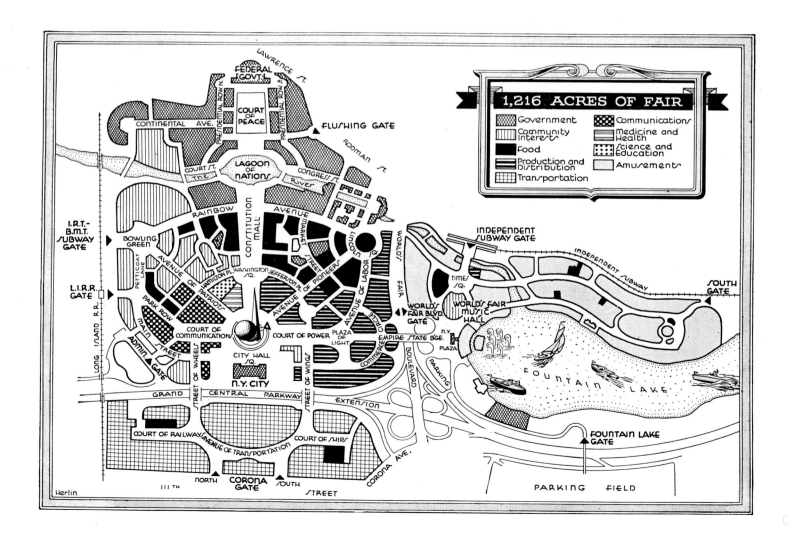

James Earle Fraser's statue of George Washington in his inaugural robes stood on a 12-foot pedestal and rose to a height of more than 60 feet.

specially made for it by the city. Out of a fifty-year accumulation of ashes and a salt marsh, the ground was created. Underground pipes and conduits were laid—enough to serve a city of 1,000,000. Ten thousand shade trees were brought from parts as far away as Massachusetts. After that the construction of the 300 buildings of the Fair began. At the peak of the job, 25,000 men were at work.

Built and operated by a non-profit organization headed by Grover A. Whalen, president, the Fair represents an investment of $26,700,000 by the City of New York, $6,200,000 by the State, $3,000,000 by the Federal Government, $30,000,000 by foreign governments and $42,000,000 by the Fair Corporation. Exhibitors' expenditures make up the rest of the total of $155,000,000.

When the Fair is over and the site becomes a park, the profits, if any, will go to the city, the state and educational and charitable institutions.

The Fair, an ancient institution, dates back to the fifth century, but no exposition in history has cost as much, offered as much or made accommodations for as many visitors as the New York World's Fair. The current show is, in a manner of speaking, a library of Time, Space, History, Industry, Art and High Jinks—the universe in full color with a wide perspective on the future to boot. The fairgoer can see and do incredible things.

A sightseer with good wind, and the inclination, can journey around 90 per cent of the earth's inhabited surface, take a flight into interstellar space and return; stand in Yesterday, Today and Tomorrow—all within two hours and within the boundaries of the Fair's 1,216 acres.

Six babies were born at Chicago's Century of Progress. New York's Fair, unless the actuaries have slipped up in their arithmetic, should be the birthplace of twelve to eighteen babies. The Fair's medical staff is prepared to handle at least that many.

The total paved area at the Fair is equivalent to sixty miles of two-lane highways.

Mountains were moved to prepare the Fair site. The expostion stands on a primeval bog that had been used for many years as a city dump. One heap of ashes 100 feet high, locally known as Mount Corona, was moved to make way for the Fair.

To remove the ashes for the Fair site 30,000 men worked 190 days. They removed 7,000,000 cubic yards of fill, used 800,000 cubic yards of top soil and built two great artificial lakes. The ash removal job alone cost $2,200,000.

More than 15,000,000 hot dogs and 15,000,000 hamburgers, as exposition statisticians figure it, will be sold

by any of the three city subway systems, by the Long Island Railroad, by many motor parkways, and by boat.

The ten gateways will be open daily at 9 A. M.; the exhibition buildings at 10 A. M. Curfew hour is 10 P. M. except in the Amusement Zone, which will stay in session till 2 A. M.

Gate charges are 75 cents for adults, 25 cents for children. On special days to be announced each week children will get in for 10 cents. The greater part of the main show is wide open to the public without further charge. A few of the industrial shows ask a nominal fee. Admission to the attractions in the Amusement Zone runs from 10 to 40 cents.

It will be an easy Fair to look at and get around in. The many diagonal streets and the grouping of exhibits save legwork. Intramural buses, tractor trains, taxi-chairs and push-chairs reduce the strain for the foot-weary. And there are resting spots and 50,000 benches —most of them in the shade.

A three-year task: To build the Fair has taken three years. Flushing Meadows Park, with its two lakes, was

on the grounds. These, strung necklace fashion, would reach from New York to London. Rolls to match would pave all the city streets.

Five hundred motion pictures will be run off daily in fifty auditoria. There will be full-length Hollywood features, animated cartoons, educational, scenic and industrial films, many in color.

More than a quarter-million people can be fed in the Fair's eighty restaurants in a single night. Statisticians estimate that the restaurants should peddle $18,000,000 worth of victuals, refreshment stands and bars about $4,647,000 worth.

The 300 buildings on the grounds cost between $40,000,000 and $50,000,000. Building contracts, in many cases, provide for destruction of these edifices as soon as the Fair ends. World of Here-Today-Gone-Tomorrow.

In the amusement zone visitors can jump 250 feet from a parachute tower and be sure of a safe landing. Wire guides make it foolproof.

In the Time and Space Auditorium the sightseer can outdo Buck Rogers; soar into celestial vastness at 480,000,000,000,000,000,000,000 miles an hour, through meteoric showers, see Earth drop away and vanish; get a close-up of a solar eclipse and intimate glimpses of Venus, the Moon, Saturn and Mars without taxing his blood pressure or disturbing his hair.

The job of preparing the Fair was equivalent to building an entirely new city of 800,000 population on an uninhabited spot.

Murder will be committed at the Fair several times each day with the help of the police. The murders will be immediately solved, though, through fingerprints and scientific scrutiny of clues at the police laboratory. It's part of the New York City Police Exhibit.

The beam on the Star Pylon is equivalent to 1,000,000 100-watt lamps.

A manufacturer of playing cards will show the world's most complete collection of "Devil's picture books," including a deck made 300 years ago from human scalps. You can pass this hand, if you like.

The greatest migration of living trees, some of them fifty-five and sixty feet high, was accomplished to give the Fair natural shade and decoration. The trees were carted an average of sixty miles from Maryland, Pennsylvania, Connecticut, New Jersey and upper New York State in specially designed trucks. A total of 10,000 trees was brought in, some of them up to twenty-five to thirty tons each.

In addition to planting 10,000 live trees, Fair gardeners planted 1,000,000 bulbs (gift from Holland), 274,000 beddings plants, 400,000 pansies, 500,000 hedge plants, 250 acres of greensward. One workman sat up all night with an ailing chestnut tree and begged for more fertilizer for it. As a boy he had known the tree in his home town.

More than $12,000,000 was spent for underground improvements, much of which the visitor will never see— for thirteen miles of gas mains, fifteen miles of water mains, thirty miles of sewers and fifteen miles of electric cable housing.

George Gershwin, who wrote the music for the Fair's theme song, "Dawn of a New Day," never heard the lyric. Ira Gershwin, his brother, wrote it after George Gershwin's death.

Ten entrance gates will admit 160,000 visitors an hour, at peak hours.

From revolving balconies in the 200-foot Perisphere you can look down, as from an altitude of two miles, on

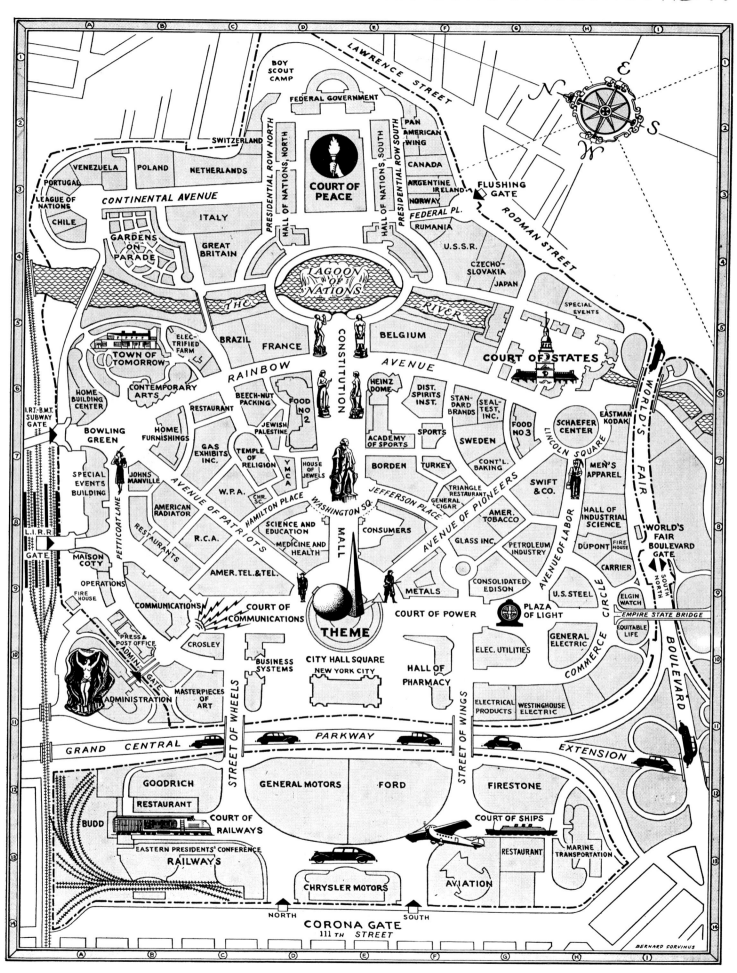

BERNARD CORVINUS

a metropolis of 250,000 souls; see dawn, dusk, noon and night and how they affect the whole scene—all within six minutes, real as life.

Without a sneeze you can step from a snow-covered ski jump in Sun Valley, Idaho, into Southern Rhodesia; trek by day and night through jungle damp and a tropical storm with real lightning; see and hear Victoria Falls pouring 60,000 gallons of water over its spillway every minute. The water's real, the roar of the Falls a sound effect.

An entire forest was destroyed to convert the Flushing marsh into solid foundation. Seven hundred and fifty-eight miles of piling were driven into the ground. The Trylon and Perisphere combined weigh 13,500,000 pounds and rest on 1,000 timber piles.

Ireland's exhibit, in a shamrock-shaped building, has transplanted chunks of "the ould sod" for its lawns and gardens, and water from the River Shannon and the Lakes of Killarney for miniature versions of those places.

Each day at noon, in the Polish exhibit, a trumpeter will sound the "heynal," a tribute to a bugler who sounded the call 700 years ago when Genghis Khan marched on Cracow.

Twenty-six Eastern railroads invested over $3,000,000 for their exhibit. For the outdoor display, 3,600 feet of track were laid out and 200,000 square feet of exhibit space were required for the indoor, or roundhouse stuff. The model railroad, 160 feet wide and 40 feet deep, is the world's largest; it is part of a diorama including 500 pieces of rolling stock, with 300,000 feet of wire in the signal and control system.

Two hundred tons of paint were used on Fair buildings.

Living actors in a universe all their own, magnified to 2,000 times normal size, will cavort on a five-foot screen for the edification of visitors. It's done with the micro-vivarium, a combination microscope and projection lantern in the Westinghouse exhibit. The actors are inhabitants of a drop of water.

Fair doctors (forty of them aided by seventy nurses) will handle more than 40,000 cases of one kind or another, according to aches-and-pains statisticians.

In the New York Zoological Society building electric eels will ring bells and light lamps—unless they get temperamental and refuse to do their stuff.

The World's largest steam locomotive, 130 feet long, weighing 519 tons, built for the Pennsylvania Railroad will keep running at seventy-five miles an hour at the Fair—on friction bearings. Actually it won't move one inch; just mark time at high speed.

Gentlemen inclined to see things after the first or second round are advised to keep out of the Men's Apparel Quality Guild exhibition. The ceiling there is an aquarium alive with goldfish.

Twin prows in the Hall of Marine Transportation are each thirty feet higher than the nose of the Normandie.

The parking zone, covering 215 acres, has room for 43,000 cars.

Every three days a fresh cargo of orchids plucked out of Venezuelan jungles will be flown to the Fair for exhibition.

One billion dollars (if the statisticians are borne out) will be spent in Greater New York during the Fair, as follows: $250,000,000 for entertainment; $200,000,000 for housing; $250,000,000 for food and liquor; $100,000,000 for transportation; $50,000,000 for personal service; $10,000,000 for communication; $140,000,000 for merchandise.

The forecourt of the Government Building in the Federal Exhibit Area has room for 50,000 parading troops.

The Fair police force will include 1,000 patrolmen, 30 sergeants, 3 captains, G-men, city detectives and special details of New York's "finest" will swell the force on special occasions to as much as 3,000 and more.

A mature orange grove, just so much orange juice on the hoof, was transported all the way from Florida for that state's exhibit.

More than 300,000 persons at one time can see the 231 shows in the Amusement Zone. This zone covers two square miles.

A real skeleton in the Hall of Man, Medical and Health Building, moves his joints—and explains each action to the audience. It's done with a recording device.

In the Exhibit Area, there are about 200 separate buildings. The Fair statisticians haven't figured out what these buildings and their contents represent in cash—but the total is well over $100,000,000. The foremost of the world's designers have labored to present in the hundreds of exhibits the stories of industry, government, science and the arts. Their aim was to be informative without being dull—to interest as well as to educate. They have achieved that aim.

CHAPTER THREE

A Day at the Fair: An Eyewitness Account

The pavilion of the Union of Soviet Socialist Republics was designed by Boris Iofan and Karo S. Alabian. At 269 feet, its central pylon was the second tallest structure at the Fair. The star in the hand of the 79-foot-high stainless-steel statue glowed red at night and was an officially designated aviation beacon, warning low-flying planes of its presence. Although meant to glorify the Soviet worker, the statue was not received ideologically by workmen at the Fair who dubbed it "Big Joe" and "The Bronx Express Straphanger."

Commentators wrote millions of descriptive words about the 1939 New York World's Fair for newspapers, magazines, newsreels, and radio broadcasts, but none more evocatively than Edmund Gilligan. His "Report of a Subway Explorer of His Trip to a Magic City," filed for The Sun, *captures the excitement, beauty, and magnificence that was the World of Tomorrow. Fifty years after they were written, Gilligan's words remind us that there was once a time, not so very long ago, when people believed not only in a tomorrow, but in a better tomorrow.*

New York City. The subway. The Flushing I.R.T. from Times Square to Willets Point.

The door closes and the subway train begins its run. It rolls at its usual pace out of the station, goes on to the next, and glides to a stop. Guards intone the familiar names and numbers, open the doors, and close them. People come in and go out. The train speeds beneath half the city and then flashes into open air, climbs above the roofs and chimneys of the Borough of Queens and carries on, clackety-clack. The guard, who has been gazing dully to the north, turns now to the south, steps nearer the window. Passengers turn their heads, too, and look out over the sea of Corona's flat roofs.

Far away, on the dim horizon, a bright gleam breaks through the mist. It is like the flash of a white bird's wing, but a flash which repeats itself and becomes a steady glow as if a ray of the sun had found some bright thing hidden in the vapor-laden air. The sun is joined by a wind out of the west. There's a scurry in the sky, a whirling of clouds, a movement of fog and shadow. This is the moment and the place for the first sight of the World of Tomorrow, the first glimpse of its chief symbols. It comes in an unveiling of the earth itself, comes in a glorious sweep of sunlight illuminating the flat land.

A slender white obelisk thrusts itself out of the arc of the earth into the streaming clouds. It is the Trylon—a flight away from the bonds of rock and clay, away from the burdens of stone and wood and iron. The eye speeds with that soaring line to the top which tapers away into the gull track. The mind races on to a tremendous height, so strong is the feeling of upward flight that it compels. A lowering cloud passes. Its shadow dapples the gray spaces of the upper surface as gulls swoop down and wheel round and round the distant spire.

Swiftly the train speeds on. Girders of the "el" flash between the eye, hiding a vast, wave-like splurge of many colors, giving but one short glimpse of that other great symbol of the fair—the Perisphere, a great beautiful ball of steel, huge as a city block, yet so cunningly set in the earth that it seems ready to float gently away for a flight to Mars, a captive balloon for giants to ride in.

The train door opens again. Take twenty steps forward into the broad plaza, and then—the enthralling vista of the fair unfolds itself, rolls out in a vast, sunspangled, glittering wave of buildings, avenues, lagoons, and gardens. A great league-long wave of the tropical Pacific it seems, white foam at the beginning, then curving, springing walls of rich green and blue beyond the heaving crest, flowing upward in a thousand brilliant plays of color and form. Forging against the leaping waves are two vast prows in the distance. Great white horses leap in the shadows of the prows. Heroic gods and goddesses stand in noble array. A huge star beams from a tower top. A huge statue of a man looms against the morning sky.

A few steps more and then—fountains fling misty clouds of water high, and dancing shadows of fountains fall and tremble on beds of flowers and flowered walks of green turf. Roses and violets and pansies, tulips and hyacinths and blooming hedge plants—all these and thousands of green-leafed trees send their fragrances into the salty air. Dogwood blossoms gleam against the shadows. Birches show their beauty amid rows of evergreens. All the beautiful trees of America are here in flush of spring beauty. Even the weeping willow leans over a lagoon there to the east.

Yet there is something more, something that escapes the glance at first. There's some quality,

breathtaking and yet mysterious, as if the whole splendid, cheerful array had a mystical meaning not to be put into thought or words. Once again the Trylon and the Perisphere strike their notes. The buildings near and far, wherein the wonders are stored, lift the eye with soaring lines and symphonies of color.

It is this examination of the grand scheme of the fair that gives away the secret of the colors, each flower bed, each flowering tree, even the very colors of the infinite numbers of Holland tulips—all these shades and hues have been blended with the color harmony of the buildings. The colors mixed by man are here set off and aided by the infinite gradations of colors mixed by nature. The Perisphere and Trylon, which sometimes seem gray when seen from the distance, now show themselves to be a pure white. Away from the Theme Center run the avenues, each having its own color. One is a street with blue, a blue that begins with a shade like a robin's egg and ends far off with a surge of aquamarine. Another begins with the color of rosebuds and rises through the chromatic scale to a sweep of ruby.

For each of these man-made colors—painted or blown into high walls of glass or mixed with clay—there is a color in the flower beds and the gardens. Lavender heliotrope and red phlox play their parts amid the yellow and blue areas. The dogwood flowers and other pink and white blooms lend light and grace to the evergreens in

their rows and parks. Now, in the full tide of the morning sun, all these flowers and trees join in a beautiful shimmering and melding of colors that it seems cannot be excelled for brilliance.

Thus the day at the fair begins. The natural fear that it couldn't be quite so wonderful has gone away. There's an assurance in the great exactitude, even of the flower beds, that all goes well with the mighty enterprise, that there won't be a dropped stitch in the magic carpet. This feeling of confidence and assurance is so strong that if one little Holland bulb turns its head the wrong way, or isn't blushing sufficiently, you would feel justified in knocking at Grover Whalen's door over there and saying: "Mr. Fair President, how can such a terrible thing happen?" But there's nothing wrong. Smoothness and beauty are the dominant notes. These are the qualities that strike the eye, but the brain sees that under the amazing surface there is a genius of organization, that the fair is well started and will roll merrily along.

Now for the tour, the eager stepping from point to point, the hard task of choosing, the task of deciding: What's next? The question's already answered. There's a magnet drawing every man, woman, and child that comes, halting and wondering, into that first wide plaza. The magnet is the Trylon. Eyes turn up to its slender beauty time and time again. But there is no way of climbing up into that vast interior. This entrance leads into the companion piece, the great Perisphere. Inside the chromium doors, a moving stairway moves upward in perfect silence. The rider ascends between gleaming walls of steel, feeling a strange sensation, one of rising to infinite height from the earth. At the upper level two tremendous circular platforms begin to revolve. Far above, the ceiling of the Perisphere curves in a sweep, giving that same feeling of flight, making it seem that one is actually in a balloon on a skyward rise.

Then the eye turns downward and there is the theme of all these wonders, the community of the World of Tomorrow—Democracity, a mighty metropolis, done in model scale. Forests and streams and wide meadows stretch away to the horizon. Farms and homes stand beside gleaming streams. Factories stand in special areas, and around the city itself are rows of garden apartments. A great river winds to the sea. The daylight wanes and thousands of lights appear in the city. Windows in the homes glow. Lamps gleam on the river. Searchlights pierce the darkness of the harbor. Far overhead the stars come out, one by one, then in great companies. A strain of music plays, thin, flutelike, far away. This swells suddenly into a chorus of thousands of voices, singing a triumphant march, a thunderous paean of victory. High in the glowing heavens, strange, dim figures appear. They advance, then change into ten

marching columns, converging, in the tumult of rolling song, upon the metropolis.

Men of all degrees stride forward in those legions of tomorrow. Miners with lamps, engineers with blueprints, teachers with books, farmers, businessmen—all looking forward to the city waiting to receive them. With arms upraised, faces shining in the blaze of color, the paraders sing the hymn of tomorrow. In matchless precision this great throng advances until at last a circle of heroic figures is formed under the vault of heaven. The music mounts to its climax and begins to diminish. A glorious burst of many-colored lights floods the scene. The music becomes fainter, thinner. Streamers of light break from the zenith and pour down upon the fabulous scene. Day begins to break and the marchers vanish. The first big show of the fair is at an end. The spectator passes to the Helicline, a long slowly descending spiral walkway, which leads back to earth again and out of the strange, inspiring dream of Democracity.

It's noon outside. The sun's standing above the apex of the Trylon. Newer and more glorious tints of color are brought out by the sun in its advance. Rays of light spring from the fountains. The pleasant breeze from the ocean stirs new fragrances from the multitude of flowers. Here, from the center of the fair, one sees the great names of

the exhibitors held against the sky: Ford, General Motors, Chrysler, Bell Telephone, Edison, General Electric, Westinghouse—all are there, each set over a handsome building, housing their offerings to America, their fascinating samples of the time to come.

Great murals—and with the flying figures of the artists' imagination, painted in pastels and more vivid hues—stand in the commanding positions. On the façade of the Communications Building is the fantasy that struck the mind of Eugene Savage, the artist, when he came to the great task of painting the story of messages, the progress of the art of speech from the age of myth to the age when myths are household fixtures. Pegasus leaps forward through the blue sky and Terpsichore, the symbol of the dance, illustrates the dance of the intellect among words. Smoke signals by North American Indians rise and curl over the prairie. A radio wave band turns into the figures of three Muses, hurling themselves toward Earth. Earth, as in the fable, rests upon the back of great Atlas, who, in the strain of his labor, looks into a mirror held up to him by the figure of Truth.

Everywhere the faces of the great buildings hold such murals and buildings of a kind never before seen. One building has murals of gleaming steel, steel cut into sculptures and set against the walls. Others are sculptures of new chemicals and there are glittering murals of spun glass, miracles of the glassmaker's art. In that roving glance over the general scene—that look before the next door opens—hundreds of such murals and scores of heroic sculptures meet the eye.

It's hard to turn away from the brilliant exterior, but there is so much to be seen that the step must be made. Turn to the right, stroll across the Court of Power and there's the Electric Utilities Building. Here, of all places in the fair, one expects to see the last word in lighting—

Administration Building.

but what's this? A door opens out of the main hall and instead of brilliantly shaded lights and reflections in pools of glass, there's something very strange, indeed. Gloom and shadows and darkness. You'd need the eyes of an old-fashioned cat to get around in this place. It seems that there must be a mistake, that this is an unfinished part of the fair. In fact, it's old and dingy enough to be part of ancient Flushing. Cobblestones! Can it be possible? Yes, that's exactly what they are. It's like Cornhill in Boston. And these weird, fitful, guttering lamps? They look like gas lamps of the old time. And that's right, too.

The door closes softly. The music of the World of Tomorrow fades and so the images of tomorrow fade, plunging horses and glittering murals, flowers and trees, Trylon and Perisphere. All these run from the memory and, in this gentle gloom, there comes back the World of Yesterday. Yes, that's the secret. Here's the sharp contrast, a sample of what yesteryear was, a sample of what we've left behind. It tells the story of how far we've come and, by implication, tells us how far we have yet to go.

One stands in a street, a street of 1891. An evening breeze rustles the leaves overhead. A leaf falls from the bough, turns in the still air, drops lightly to the ground. Voices murmur behind the dimity curtains of the home above the stores. It's after supper and the children are asleep. There's the theater, and a man—looks like the town barber—stands in front of it, peering closely at posters of the Rehan stock company. A lady, stately in her long skirts, opens a door, looks out and closes it again.

Look down into the kitchen of the home next to the theater! There's a wooden tub there with an ancient washboard thrust into it and a pile of laundry waiting. Evidently tomorrow will be wash day in that house. A gas fixture on the wall sends out a golden beam of light. And there's the apothecary's shop. Vials of colored liquids adorn his windows, and two little electric bulbs are burning there. The druggist is apparently the first customer in town for this new-fangled electricity stuff. And here's the Edison office. They're making a fuss, too, about something or other. There's the sign: Tenth anniversary of the incandescent lamp. And there's another sign saying that this single industry employed 8,500 men throughout the country last year. Overhead there's a maze of wires, scores of them stretched on telegraph poles. And this Edison manager—he's got a big horseshoe of flowers in his window with a ribbon on it, saying: Good luck!

And then there's some strange affair nailed onto the wall of his office, another of those tricky things—a telephone. And strange talk, too, as the manager shouts into it. Says he can hear a man fifty miles away just as

plain as if he was leaning out the window. Claims the day will come when a fellow can just pick up that receiver part, which you put to your ear, and speak to San Francisco right away. Moreover, he's ready to bet that he'll be heard, too. More than that, he's already bragging about telephoning across the Atlantic to London some day! Impossible. . . .

Leave the world of yesterday and come out into the Court of Power. Perhaps the answer to that Edison man's prophecy of 1891 lies in one of these buildings. And there's one that seems to fit the bill—the Consolidated Edison Building, adorned with flowing fountains, throwing their changing shadows on the imposing walls. Pass through the entrance into the main hall and there's the city of today—New York itself portrayed in a huge diorama, a block long and higher than a three-story building. Tall buildings fill the horizon. Factories and stores and highways—the whole metropolis is set forth on a model scale, done so cleverly that the illusion is complete. It is like looking at the city itself from the East River.

The natural light fades from the sweep of the sky and the evening comes slowly on. One by one, then by the tens and hundreds and thousands, the lights come on. A beacon gleams far above the rows of apartments, where homeowners turn on their lights and begin their evening hours. An elevated train speeds from uptown. The darkness increases and at last becomes complete, leaving the whole city glowing with myriads of lights. Elevators rise in the skyscrapers and beams of light pierce the darkness as the motor traffic rolls across great bridges. It is a living city, full of action.

All the things the Edison manager of 1891 spoke of are here in reality. There's a glimpse into an apartment, high above the streets. Gas cooks the dinner, electricity makes the coffee, runs the radio, brings the message that dad will be a little late. The whole economy of the home within the city and the part that modern power takes in that economy are portrayed. That washtub in the kitchen is nowhere to be seen. Even the dishes are out of sight, already in the electric dishwasher. The fitful, dim gaslights are gone and, in their place, comes the steady glow of bulbs.

And now the darkness grows even greater. The sky clouds over. Late workers in the high buildings turn on more lights. A storm is coming over the city, adding its gloom to the shadows of night. Music foretells the approach of the storm. Thunder rumbles and then the first faint flash of lightning cuts across the horizon. The demands on the electric equipment are increasing, too.

Traffic lights gleam and blink. More and more trains hurry through the subways as the rush hour traffic approaches its peak. The storm descends but still "The City of Light" remains glowing with millions of lamps, unaffected by the storm that rages in the sky.

The storm passes, the evening passes, and bedtime approaches. The lights begin to go out. First the tall buildings go dark. Fewer and fewer are the trains streaming out of the darkness to the long reaches of the elevated. The motor cars and taxicabs dwindle in number. And then the lights in the thousands of homes go out. At last the city is asleep. Of course, lights always are going. Students and playboys keep odd hours. Hotels and roof gardens still send out their bright and colored gleams.

But don't get the impression from all these wonders done by the engineers that the fair is only a show of mechanical marvels. Far from it. Of course, art is present in all these colors, shapes, and lighting. All the fine arts, all that treasure trove of painting and jewels and coins and books—where are they? This way. Once more toward the Lagoon of Nations and then, by a turn here, into the Japanese Pavilion, made as the ancient Shinto shrines were made.

The Japanese are the master garden makers. They can shut the world off by a tree set in a certain way, can induce calm in the hurried soul by a vine dropping over a rustic bridge. Here they've done it. Pools and sparkling cascades and the quiet of waters flowing slowly. And in this room, there's a fortune in pearls, the sort of pearls that divers bring up from the oyster beds of the Japanese islands. Cultured pearls. Thousands of them have been cunningly put together into this—an exact model of the Liberty Bell of Philadelphia, even to the famous crack itself. Tomorrow, if you'd like to take tea in the style of the Japanese tea cult, this is the place. Some of these charming young ladies, with their high hair combs and bright kimonos, will show you how it's made and how it is sipped.

Step outside and go down Presidential Row North. That trilling sound is an excellent example of Swiss yodeling and it comes from the Swiss pavilion, where we can climb part way up an Alp and spend a while in a Swiss cabin. It's a cheesemaker's cabin and it presents an excellent opportunity to find out how Swiss cheese is made—including the holes. And then you see the great display of laces and embroideries and the famous Swiss watches.

These two halls—the Japanese and the Swiss—are just the beginning of an unprecedented display of the arts and culture of sixty peoples, a display that warrants days of time to enjoy properly, but there's one thing that can't be put off. That's the British pavilion. There are the treasures of England: the Magna Charta itself, a replica of the crown jewels, and pieces of ceremonial and presentation plate, lent by the King himself, who will be with us shortly and will be able to see for himself that everything is just so. It is to the Dean and Chapter of Lincoln Cathedral that we owe the presence of the great charter, a document forever associated with the idea of freedom. And there—decorated with shields and arms—is a large panel showing the ancestry of George Washington. It reveals that he was descended not only from King John, who signed the charter, but also from nine of the barons who became sureties for its execution.

Through all these pavilions there are beautiful works of art, but the grand collection of all the masters is farther away in that building on the Street of Wheels which is called "Masterpieces of Art." All the great periods of European art from the Middle Ages to 1800 are represented here by paintings that have been valued at $30,000,000. They come from the Louvre, the Uffizi Gallery in Florence, the National in London, and the Rijksmuseum in Amsterdam. Here are shown the originals of the many reproductions so popular in America. Some of the artists are Da Vinci, Raphael, Michelangelo, Titian, and, among the French artists, the brothers Le Nain and Claude Lorraine.

That's a part of the fair's storehouse of art. And here's one more art, that of entertainment, which has had its share of attention by the fair's directors. The amusement area is just about the biggest circus there ever was. Even the Ubangi tribesmen, who used to startle people in sideshows with their peculiar lips, are on the job again. There are penguins and tigers and thousands of other beasts and birds, but the truth of it is that—just like the circus—this part of the show needs the gaiety of a big crowd, the gaping faces and the cries of astonishment to give it the right flavor.

So, Frank Buck and Eleanor Holm and the wonders of the jungle and the deep are left until another day.

Outside again and the sun is passing over in precisely the orderly fashion that Grover Whalen requires. But what's that? Thunder? In bright daylight? The thunderclaps are coming from the left, from the General Electric building, a structure decorated with a sizable flash of lightning. Made of stainless steel, it's the sign of the whole exhibit, its theme sign: taming and guiding and harnessing the enormous force of electricity. This is Steinmetz Hall. It's a huge room, and from the balcony, running from end to end, you can watch the incredible show below. A group of enormous columns stand at either end of the floor. They are as big as the stacks of ocean liners and made of black, shiny metal with wide silver bands. A space of about fifty feet separates the two groups. From each inner tower a spear-shaped electrode points across the space. Young men, faintly seen, move among the columns. There are other men high in a cage set against the opposite wall. They lean over boards of gleaming instruments, panels of copper, panels lined with switches that send bright beams of light into the increasing gloom. The lights fade. A voice shouts far off at the other end. Near at hand another man answers. They talk a scientific language barely understood by most people in the hall. Then a man nearby turns and speaks. "We are about to imitate Nature herself," he says. "We are going to have a bit of lightning and a spot of thunder. Not enough to make your hair curl or deafen anybody, but enough for our purpose." And what's his purpose? "By reproducing the conditions that exist in a real thunderstorm, General Electric tests its equipment. Transformers and such things must be made so that thunder and lightning in the cities and countryside can't harm them. They keep on functioning whether it storms or not."

Great glass tubes on the other side of the massive columns begin to glow. This is a preliminary test to see if all is as it should be. There's a shout and then comes a bang—just like a rifle shot. It's nothing much, just the working of the grounded wire that takes off the initial release of power. Again a shout and once more the rifle shot. The engineers exchange a few words and then the signal comes that the great performance is to take place.

The signal is a shout and then a tremendous bolt of violet flame shoots from the electrodes and there's a thunderous blast of sound. The flash is so quick that it's necessary to keep the eyes fixed right on the spear points to see it leap across the gap. But the sight is beautiful, exciting, crowd pleasing. The calm General Electric person who looks on from the balcony smiles comfortably and declares that 50,000 volts danced across that space. This is 1939 and anything is possible.

From G. E. to G. M. Across the Bridge of Wheels to the future according to General Motors. The Futurama, housed in a mighty building designed by Norman Bel Geddes, complete with great winding ramps, done in dazzling colors, and with curving roofs that speed toward the sky. Within this building, we are transported twenty-one years ahead in time to 1960, the year General Motors has picked for the realization of America's "Highways and Horizons," the name of its chief exhibit. Under these amazing roofs the company projects a basic theme of highway progress and possible trends in motor transportation facilities. On entering by one of the three ramps which go down into a great room, there is an illusion by lighting effects of looking out into infinite space. Seemingly suspended in the air is an enormous map of the country, more than 100 feet long. Matched by a voice speaking from some secret place, the map changes before the eye and tells the story of the highways and horizons of the present. Problems are solved and the great problems of the future, multiplying as the number of cars increases, are also discussed.

Then, smoothly approaching in the subdued light, appears a procession of large chairs, winged in the old-fashioned way. You step onto a moving floor, which goes forward at the same speed as the moving chairs, and you take a seat. Here's something so new and wonderful that a new and rather wonderful word has been coined to describe it: futurama. The fair boasts panoramas, dioramas, and one or two others, but this is a departure from all the "ramas" past, present, and forgotten.

The chairs move on. Instantly a voice begins to speak right inside the chair, a device that passeth understanding because it is so synchronized that, as the scenes changes, the voice begins to describe the next one. But the people riding a few chairs behind are still hearing the description of the scene you have passed. The electrical engineers who built it for General Motors say that it is the most complex sound system ever devised. And it is: It is capable of delivering 150 descriptive talks at the same time, all synchronized to the 600 moving chairs. This is a creation that the Edison man of '91 never even dreamed of.

The chairs slide onward and presently the first vista of the futurama unfolds itself as it might be seen from a low-flying plane, speeding up a beautiful valley. Miniature towns and cities lie there, set forth in marvelous detail. Factories send up their smoke and electric derricks work in the yards. Hundreds of thousands of homes—farms and apartments and country estates—lie in great cities, in towns, and in rural scenes. Rivers flow to the sea, suspension bridges cross them. And everywhere there is the constant never-ending flow of automobile traffic. There are 50,000 small-scale cars in view at various times and 10,000 of them are in actual operation. They speed at fifty miles an hour and more on special lanes for fast traffic. They stop under control towers and wind over bridges of several decks.

The illusion of traveling hundreds of miles at vibrationless speed in some amazing plane of the future is complete. It's almost like a guided tour by air over the continent. The chairs mount sometimes at a sharper degree of curvature and then go evenly down into a lower level. Step by step the whole world of the future passes beneath. Streamlined trains, daring in design, slide into tunnels under high mountains and emerge to climb through the snowy peaks. Great transport planes lie in the airports while automobiles speed between railroads and airfields.

In precise accents, changing without a fault from scene to scene, the sound system expounds the theory of each development, tells why experts think these things must come to pass. In this fashion, the traveling chairs pass over a track more than a third of a mile long—and then comes the most dramatic representation of all: we are given a view of ninety blocks of the metropolis of the future. The voice describes the express boulevards and feeder streets. An elevated sidewalk system separates pedestrians and vehicular traffic. The final view of the city is a single street intersection and its buildings, and this is suddenly enlarged so that one can see people moving in the elevated sidewalks and cars on the street level. Even the shop windows have their signs and decorations of the future.

The tour ends. The chair turns quickly, and suddenly the rider sees the city intersection again, this time the real thing, not in miniature. His chair moves in a semicircle and he steps to an elevated sidewalk, the pavement of tomorrow. He takes his first wondering steps on a sidewalk that might well be a common thing in 1960. He looks down and sees the automobiles below him. A real building rises four stories above him. General Motors has brought him back to Flushing, 1939.

And now—television. At the RCA building, a pretty little pavilion, round as a cheesebox and nicely designed in red and white. Television—radio with pictures. Here are the machines. Beautiful cabinets, too, and there's the screen up in back there, just like a motion picture show.

The camera's ready in New York and the sending antennas are all set. Turn the switch and here we are in Flushing and seeing a bus on Fifth Avenue! A miracle of the future already operating in the present.

Afternoon moves along. Already the high roof of glass, in the rampart that looks eastward, has caught a sign of night crossing the Atlantic. A deeper green, rich as the trough of an ocean wave, tints the beautiful tower. March westward, then, with the wheel of the sun, pass up the Street of Wings and over the Bridge of Wings. There, under the name of Ford, is one of the most extraordinary murals in the fair. Set in the entrance, between the walls of glass, is the great mobile mural designed by Henry Billings. Engine parts, done on a giant scale, are set on revolving bases. A cylinder is indicated in the center and there is an electric spark just as in a Ford motor. The spark explodes, the piston moves, and the instant action passes among the parts.

Inside, in the main hall, another wonder of the new time. Not only a lesson in the intricate economy of mass production, but an excellent lesson in physics. There it is: a revolving mountain, going round and round smoothly and without even a mite of noise. Not an iota. At its top there's a platform on which a group of completed cars stand. On each of the great steps coming down to the wide base there's a group of alert little figures, men and women and children. There are little farms and railroads and mines and plantations. All the workers are at attention: picks are held in mid-air, goads stop over the oxens' heads, ore cars pause at the curve.

A signal comes and then these husky little figures get to work like so many dwarfs in an old story. A brown-skinned cowboy on a pinto horse whirls his rope toward a family of cows. There's a little calf that thinks it's all play and bobs up and down by his mother. Next to him stands a man ripping cork from a tree and handing it to his helper. Then there's a pair of muscular toy-men striking hard in an asbestos mine, shoveling the stuff into cars. The car moves away, runs up the mountain, turns into a tunnel, and arrives at the factory. And one after the other, eighty-seven different animated displays on that revolving mountain show the progression of raw materials from earth to finished automobile.

There are a score of other fascinating sights to see under the Ford roof: "The Road of Tomorrow," in which cars roll half a mile on a great spiral ramp, and a Garden Court, where music plays and you may rest a while.

Over now to the Railroad building on the Avenue of Transportation, where we find the last word in streamlined locomotives. Weighs 526 tons, they say, and if there were a single track to Mars it would get there in no time. There goes the engineer in his overalls and with a smart bandanna around his neck, according to tradition, al-

though he doesn't really need it in that modern cab. No cinders there. It's as neat and cozy as a glass apartment in the world of 1960. He climbs in, gets behind the controls, and let's 'er go. The steam hisses, the driving wheels begin to turn—great shining disks of steel. Faster and faster they whirl. Her whistle shrieks and the blast echoes from the railroad yard beyond. But the wheels aren't going anywhere. They're synchronized with wheels set in concrete down below, and no matter how fast they go they'll never get anywhere. Not until the fair's over in 1940.

Take one last glance at that beautiful streamlined affair and step into the Railroad Building, climb up this curving ramp and take a seat in the theater. "Railroads on Parade" is the name of the show. The orchestra begins. With the first melodious strains of Kurt Weill's overture, the epic of the iron horse begins. Lights fade and the crack of day—a morning of long ago in New York—floods the vast stage. A man shouts. Horses whinny and their hoofs strike the earth, and then the increasing light reveals the scene: Erie Canal, 1825.

In the grand and glorious rush of color and gallant music, the story of transportation unrolls itself. The steam engine isn't far off. In fact, there's a British locomotive on the ocean deep, coming to work in America, but for the time being there are the stage coaches, wheeling off for Boston and Philadelphia. Whips crack, scores of horses rear and plunge, and then behave themselves. Travelers in soldiers' and sailors' uniforms of the old army and navy take their places. Pretty women guide their wide skirts through the busy square. Children cling to their mothers' hands, and father, in head-of-the-family style, declares that the time is coming when a man will be able to take his family to Washington without the aid of horses and wheels.

Father is right. The ship from England comes in, and presently the music gives us Pennsylvania in 1829, and the next great character takes its place on the stage— the Lion, an English locomotive of the period, and quite large enough to haul water for the 500-ton streamliner outside. There's a golden lion's head in front of the engine and the whole thing is shipshape and Bristol fashion. The Americans of 1829 are skeptical. Will it take the place of oxen? A team of oxen is kept on hand in case the engine never makes it out of Honesdale. But it goes. The engine works. And soon the massive stage unfolds the nation's dream of transportation. Surveyors run the lines over vast territories, where hunters shot the bison to feed armies of workers. The lines to the Pacific are flung across the continent, tie by tie, rail by rail. And all to Kurt Weill's music.

Where the Central and the Union met on that grand

day in 1869, the bigwigs gather, the workmen fling their caps into the air. The women in their bonnets look on in joy and their children peer out, watching as the last blows are struck in the steel span across the continent. A man comes forward bearing a casket. Out of it comes the famous golden spike—symbol of the great completion. It is driven. The battle's over, the task done. Weill's music soars.

And now, once more outside on the fairgrounds, the eternal drama of the sunset is in the last act. The sun goes down and, in all-embracing advance, night runs over the fair. There's no moon in the dark sky. Only a star or two in the east, one gleaming dark red, the other gold. The fair's answer to the darkness is brilliant nighttime light—man-made and glowing. Thousands of lights in the buildings burn in different hues. Each row seems to have a shading of color of its own.

The Trylon and the Perisphere stand more clearly as the symbols, their dignity enhanced by the darkness coming toward them. Far up on the Trylon's western facade, a ruby light gleams. Halfway down another flashes on and gives a ruddy shine, like the unwinking eye of some great bird of mythology. A delicate change comes in the hue of the Perisphere. The pure white loses its forthrightness. A lilac-colored cloud moves upward from the earth. The misty vapor, deepening slowly to lavender, seizes the huge ball and lends it a new lightness, a new airiness.

Sweetly out of this evening silence come the gentler noises: wind among trees, waters flowing and fountains falling, rustle of leaves, murmur of the night wind among grasses and closing flowers. Far away sounds a new and greater music. In enormous volume a melody—fifes, drums, and horns, and violins—fills the evening. Suddenly the lavender tint of the Perisphere deepens into violet, an intense glow directed by hidden lamps. One knows now that the fair is beginning to fulfill its promises of light. The enormous ball rests in that violet world and then, by the magic of a battery of projectors, the illusion of movement is created. It seems to revolve, seems to swim round and round in that lovely mist. Silvery clouds appear on that curved surface and they begin to drift against its turning, like clouds of a summer evening drifting down a country landscape.

The birches and the evergreens are set off in delicate traceries by floods of soft light directed against walls. Pillars of flame rise into the night; gas flambeaux wave upward, creating endless patterns in the darkness. Crests of fountains rise into the planes of light and send off sparkling sprays.

Each avenue presents a breathless spectacle. Buildings so strangely shaped to give room to their exhibits, change from the incisive, streamlined molds of daytime to a harmonious sea of color beyond belief. Streams of pink and white flow against the sculptured plaques of the Metals Building and make silhouettes of them. A changing blue-and-white light pours from within and turns part of the wall into a shimmering fountain of glass. The high prows of the Marine Transportation Building to the south rear in a golden sea of light. The great statue over the Russian exhibit holds up a distant star, burning with a crimson hue. High in the air, captive balloons sway in myriad changing shafts of varied lights.

Yet this is not all. Deeper now the mysterious music sends forth its melody. A more solemn note of triumph and power is heard, the clamor of brasses and strings. The horns take hold and announce that there is something yet to be done. And it is to take place far down at the end of Constitution Mall, itself a bursting stream of silver and gold. Beyond that canal of brilliant vapor lies the Lagoon of Nations. A beautiful water garden by day, adorned with lilies and lily pads, it now lies glowing with the intensity of a furnace. Below this calm surface a new stream of light shoots out, and in that instant all the lamps and flames in that area go dark. At once the glow of the water increases a thousandfold in beauty, but before the eye hardly comprehends the magical change, a mist, made by magic devices hidden in the walls of the lagoon, swims out upon the water, covers its beauty with a new and softer beauty of its own. A strain of music sounds. Bugles call. A tidal wave of crimson vapor rolls over the lagoon, rolls once and vanishes, and is at once succeeded by a wave, shimmering like a cloth of gold. This, too, vanishes before an onrush of morning sky blue. In a moment of time, a flash of fire consumes the sky.

So also the flame vanishes, and in the center of the lagoon a mound of bubbling water appears. Bubbles of lavender and violet, of lilac and green and yellow. Deep in its center a fiercer color glows, again the color of molten gold. It rises slowly, overcomes the other flashing hues, and then emerges—a golden spout. Instantly it climbs, higher and higher, shedding rays all around. It becomes a streaming column of brilliant red. Twenty feet it rises, and then twenty more, and still it goes leaping toward the sky, sending down an enormous flaming waterfall. Louder and louder grows the roar of its ascension and the clatter of its fall. One hundred feet it rises, growing in splendor as it increases in size and, at last, when it climbs still farther, the glittering crest changes to a heavenly blue color.

All around it, beaten by the winds and by the force of thundering water, rainbow-colored mists flow and twist, rise and fall. The music, straining to be heard above the outcry of the tumbling waters, strikes into a melodious uproar. At this signal another jet appears in the rippling surface of the lagoon. Again a column rises and, before it has gone the height of a tall man, still another begins to form. One by one these great fountains emerge from the lagoon. Soon the sky is full of climbing, tossing, splendid, vigorous water. Water thrown into an enormous series of fountains, fountains of living, pulsing fire. Beams from searchlights form a roof of light over the

lagoon. Vapors of a hundred shades and hues drift and mix beneath the ceiling of light. There, at last, it lives: the symphony of water, color, fire, and music.

A lull of movement comes before the circles of great jets slowly open, fall outward, pour down their rosy streams at a new angle. It is like a flower from a poet's wild dream, an opening flower. The falling heaven of water becomes a wall of brilliant blue, laced with gold. A hidden force suddenly strikes at all the greater jets and molds them into a single, enormous column, and, strangely, it seems to take on the shape of a shock of corn with golden stalks and leaves and full bursting ears showing kernels of blue and red and gold, all glittering with early frost. Peals of thunder burst through the wild music. Once again the smaller jets in the outer circle leap outward, dart their glowing colors at the vast main columns. In an enormous tumult, this play continues. A new theme swells up under the roll of thunder and, in one swift instant, all this chaos vanishes.

The show is over at this fair of fairs. It is time to go home and dream of the many wonders of the World of Tomorrow still to be explored on yet another day.

CHAPTER FOUR

The Theme Center

The Trylon and Perisphere as seen from City Hall Square. Constitution Mall lies beyond the Theme Center, with the Court of Communications to the left of the Perisphere and the Court of Power to the right of the Trylon.

Not everyone liked the Trylon and the Perisphere. The Perisphere was "a big apple," said the New York *Post* when the entire city seemed to be truckin' to the rhythms of that eponymous dance craze. The *Times* called the twin symbols "the egg and the tack." The *Sun* ran an imaginary interview with the Perisphere: "What is your role, would you mind telling?" "I'm a theme, sir, that is not jelling." Robert Moses, who sniped at the 1939 fair whenever he could (and paid for his sins by presiding over the ruinous 1964 successor), remarked that "Barnum had his sacred white elephant, and every fair is entitled to at least one theme tower."

But these were four voices talking in an empty room. The rest of the world deemed the Trylon and Perisphere wonderful. As the prestigious *Architectural Forum* put it, "In New York's Trylon and Perisphere an international exposition has the first adequate trademark since Eiffel built his tower for the Paris Fair of 1889. Wallace K. Harrison and J. André Fouilhoux have provided a dominant symbol when viewed from within the Fair or from any vantage point for miles around. So great is its popularity that the design is equally familiar to every U.S. schoolboy and gaffer who see in it countless reproductions and in every conceivable form of manufactured article, from dress prints to pipes."

When Harrison and Fouilhoux were awarded the commission to design a theme center for the Fair in November 1936, they promised a design that would function as a practical exhibition hall in which the overall theme of the Fair could be dramatized. "The essence of the Fair is the expression of the life of the future," Harrison said, "and this is the idea we will try to develop in the most modern way."

This "most modern" of designs—more a monumental sculpture than a work of architecture—grew from a hairpin and a ball of putty that Harrison eventually kept among his most prized possessions. The sphere was chosen because a ball is the ideal form for enclosing the largest possible amount of space with the smallest amount of material; a tower was seen to be the natural contrasting form to a sphere. Together these two simple and natural forms appeared instantly striking and permanently impressive and were hailed upon first publication of the plans in March 1937 as "an icon of the future." As Grover Whalen said in praising the architects for a brilliant job, "We promised the world something new in Fair architecture, and here it is—something radically different and yet fundamentally as old as man's experience."

Originally, the Theme Center was to have been an exhibition rotunda surmounted by twin towers (*above left*), from which the Fair visitor could catch a glimpse of the marine amphitheatre (*above, right*) where concerts, pageants, operas, and marine shows were to be staged. While the Theme Tower was eventually abandoned, the marine amphitheatre, greatly scaled down, became the setting for Billy Rose's Aquacade.

The Trylon and Perisphere were made of 2,000 cubic yards of concrete and reinforced steel, and 3,000 tons of structural steel resting on more than 1,000 pilings of Douglas fir creosoted for durability. The total weight of the structures and their foundations was about 10,000 tons. Although no free-standing sphere had ever been built before the Perisphere and there was of consequence no engineering precedent to fall back on, construction crews managed to complete the Theme Center on schedule and without a single major accident.

A LUMINOUS WORLD

Aside from its symbolic meaning, The Theme Center served at least two practical purposes: it served as a visible locus for finding one's way about the Fair's 1,216 acres, and, from the curved Helicline, it provided a superb view of the Fair itself. As one observer wrote, "The Trylon and Perisphere are always in sight. Around them the fairgoer rotates, and from them he continually gets his bearings. When he strays from the business of seeing the Fair, they invite him back into the scheme of things. They order the Fair and somehow make it easy to see and to grasp." But there was also something intangible about the Trylon and Perisphere—its sheer beauty. As Yale historian Frank Monoghan wrote, "Here is the magnificent spectacle of a luminous world, apparently suspended in space by gushing fountains of liquid reds and blues and greens, over which clings a strange ethereal mist. An ingenious arrangement of mirror casings on which eight groups of fountains continuously play make the supporting columns invisible; while at night powerful lights project cloud patterns on the globe, and wreathing it in color mist, create the startling illusion that it is revolving like a great planet on its axis."

DEMOCRACITY

After viewing Henry Dreyfuss's imagined world of 2039 (described in the previous chapter and here illustrated), visitors to the vast interior of the Perisphere were witness to a "vision in the sky" so spectacular that it can only be called a secular apocalypse. As scores of marching and singing workers passed across the enormous dome, the sonorous voice of radio's H. V. Kaltenborn intoned: "This march of men and women, singing their triumph, is the true symbol of the World of Tomorrow . . . If the hundreds of thousands . . . and hundreds of millions . . . whom these represent—if they cannot march and work and sing together—then the World of Tomorrow cannot come into existence . . . These giant figures . . . with arms linked . . . priest and farmer and miner and housewife . . . sandhogs and baseball players and telephone operators and ministers . . . dairymen and cotton pickers and brakemen and nurses . . . men and women of all nations . . . They are marching in triumph . . . They have triumphed over chaos . . . they have built the World of Tomorrow."

Nowhere else in the entire Fair was the utopianism of the 1930s more evident.

After ascending by escalator to the interior of the Perisphere, the visitor to Democracity stepped onto one or the other of two revolving balconies (*right and opposite*) which formed huge rings seemingly unsupported in space. The platforms revolved in opposite directions and took six minutes to make a complete revolution, the show lasting just that amount of time. One hundred and twenty performances a day enabled 8,000 fairgoers to visit Democracity and its vast panoramas (*below*) daily. The accompanying musical score by William Grant Still, with lyrics by Al Stillman, was conducted by André Kostelanetz. The narrator was the popular newscaster H. V. Kaltenborn. (*Architectural Forum,* which found Henry Dreyfuss's imaginative conception nothing short of brilliant, wrote that "the commentary and musical accompaniment add nothing but confusion to the excellent original idea.")

COMMUNICATIONS

CHAPTER
FIVE

The Communications and Business Systems Zone

The Communications Building, designed by architects Francis Keally and Leonard Dean, was situated on the Court of Communications. Flanked by twin pylons 160 feet high, the building was adorned with Eugene Savage's giant mural which depicted in brilliant colors many of the world's means of communication, past and present.

On the south wall of the Communications Building was a massive carved inscription which set the idealistic tone of the Communications and Business Systems Zone:

MODERN MEANS OF COMMUNICATION SPAN CONTINENTS,
BRIDGE OCEANS, ANNIHILATE TIME AND SPACE . . .
SERVANTS OF FREEDOM OF THOUGHT AND ACTION, THEY
OFFER TO ALL MEN THE WISDOM OF THE AGES TO FREE
THEM FROM TYRANNIES AND ESTABLISH COOPERATION
AMONG THE PEOPLES OF THE EARTH.

Although the Ancients had perhaps said this better, and in fewer words ("The truth shall set you free"), most educated Americans of the 1930s, dazzled by the endless stream of scientific inventions introduced during their lifetimes, believed that modern civilization was based upon mankind's ability to communicate knowledge, sentiments, and ideas to one another and to posterity. As the *Official Guide Book* of the Fair put it, "Throughout the ages, the progress of communications was slow until the sudden advent and the universal utilization of the tremendous power of electricity. The names of great inventors in electrical fields are so familiar that we accept the results of their work as commonplace, understanding little of the transformation that each produced. The rapid and unrestricted exchange of ideas is vital to the life of mankind, and to this important field the Fair has dedicated an entire Zone."

The Focal Exhibit of the Communications Zone, located in the Communications Building, was designed by Donald Deskey and featured man himself telling the story of how he had conquered time and space. The central figure in a huge hall was an enormous human head twenty feet high. From this head emanated a voice which outlined the history of communications, while on a thirty-foot globe at the far end of the hall were flashed symbols of the postal service, the printed word, the telegraph, the radio, motion pictures, and television. On one wall was a mural by Stuart Davis based on the history of inventions which made swift communication possible. On another wall a series of animated panels showed the effects of the various means of communication on man's daily life. The entire show lasted twenty minutes.

But there was also more than idealism and entertainment to be offered in the various pavilions of the Zone. There were products—radios and telephones and business machines—to be hawked behind the gilded curtain of scientific show-business. There were cameras and encyclopedias, life insurance policies and bank safes, typewriters and Dun & Bradstreet credit reports to be sold to millions of fairgoers. For a tour of the commercial side of the Communications Zone, let us begin with the American Telephone and Telegraph Company Building on the following page.

The American Telephone and Telegraph Company Building *(above)* occupied a three-acre site immediately north of the Trylon and Perisphere. A semicircular entranceway, crowned by "The Pony Express," a sculpture group by Carl Milles representing communications of the past, led to an enormous courtyard landscaped with a small forest of pines, which soon gained a reputation as one of the coolest spots of the Fair on a hot summer's day. A statue of Mercury, long A. T. & T.'s symbol of speedy communications ("a girdle round the earth in forty seconds"), topped the exhibition hall designed by Voorhees, Walker, Foley, and Smith, a New York architectural firm that had built several prominent telephone company buildings on the East Coast. Among the telephonic wonders displayed within the interiors designed by Henry Dreyfuss was the Voice Mirror *(right),* which enabled the visitor to hear his own telephone voice. A separate entrance *(opposite page)* led to the most popular feature of the exhibit, the Demonstration Call Room, where fairgoers were chosen by lot and invited to make long distance calls to any listed telephone in the United States.

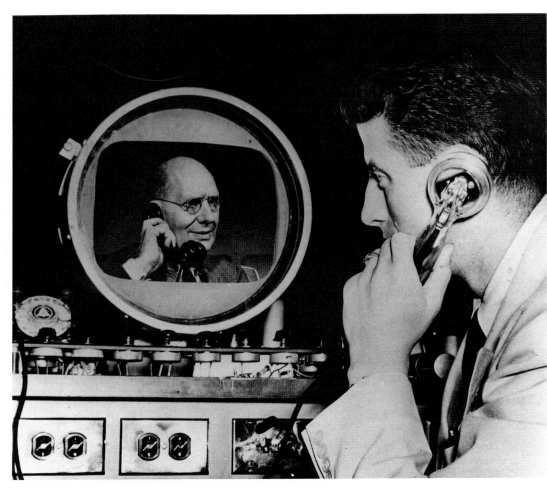

BUSINESS SYSTEMS AND INSURANCE BUILDING

One of the most beautiful buildings of the Fair, the Business Systems and Insurance Building housed a variety of not always related displays. Designed by Eric Gugler, John B. Slee, and Robert H. Bryson, the L-shaped building embodied a court, the features of which were a willow tree in its center, an extraordinary sculpted sundial—"Time," by Joseph Kiselewski—and round columns in circular formation facing Rose Court. The purpose of the buidling was to display "the complicated array of machinery which keeps the wheels of modern business turning," but the effect was only as good as the sum total of the tenant-exhibitors within. That the effect was, in fact, something of a mishmash can be seen from *The New York Times*'s attempt at finding unity in variety: "There are typewriters and elaborate computing machines and indexers. There is an exhibit of credit analysis. Life insurance is dramatized. Loan service and safes and gadgets to count and keep your money for you are here for examination. There are puppet and marionette shows and animated exhibits to emphasize the need for safety on the highways. And if the visitor wants to buy theatre tickets, have mail forwarded, cash checks, or rent a room, there is a service booth to help him out."

The most popular display in the Business Systems and Insurance Building was "the world's largest typewriter," a monster machine exhibited by the Underwood Elliott Fisher Company. The fourteen-ton, eighteen-foot replica of an Underwood Master typewriter actually typed letters three-inches high. (By 1939 enormous type-writers were nothing new. Two years earlier Ruby Keeler and Lee Dixon had danced to "Too Marvelous for Words" across a typewriter at least twice the size in Warner Bros.' *Ready, Willing and Able.* Forty chorus girls, lying on their backs within the machine, typed out the words to the song with their legs!)

The central feature of the Mosler Safe Comany exhibit was a giant vault door, thirteen feet in diameter, set against a map of the world that spelled out the company's motto, "Mosler Protects the World." The curious in Depression New York could also see photographs of America's gold reserves in Fort Knox.

The Agfa Ansco Corporation exhibit, designed by Skidmore & Owings and located in the Communications Build-ing, offered a working demonstration of a photographic darkroom and showed how giant prints could be made from tiny negatives.

THE RADIO CORPORA-
TION OF AMERICA
BUILDING

The RCA Building was designed by Skidmore & Owings
to resemble a radio tube, but the undoubted star of its
display was television. Although the visitor to the
pavilion could find almost anything he was looking for
in the field of radio and broadcasting, he came specifical-
ly to see the newest marvel of communications—radio
with pictures—and he wasn't disappointed. An unusual
architectural feature of the building was its expanse of
glass curtain walls, rare in a fair whose commercial
pavilions eschewed windows, but deemed necessary by
a company whose principal buildings (the RCA Building
in New York's Rockefeller Center and the brand-new NBC
Studios in Hollywood's Radio City of the West) were noted
for their glass-walled lobbies.

In the courtyard of the RCA Building *(opposite page)* was a 250-foot antenna tower that contained an exhibit on high-speed facsimile broadcasting, whereby news material transmitted from one point to another could be decoded by scanners.

Commercial television broadcasting in New York City began on opening day of the Fair, when the inaugural ceremonies were televised for the relatively few people who could afford several hundred Depression dollars for a set with a seven-inch screen. Mobs of fairgoers crowded the pavilion's main hall *(right)* to see the new invention in operation and to hope to be among the lucky ones who were selected to see themselves on the small screen.

Among the many products on display in the RCA Building was the Story Electronic Piano, which, novel as it was, could not compete with the Hammond Novachord, shown at the Railroads Building. Powered by 144 radio tubes, the Novachord simulated the sounds of piano, harpsichord, trumpet, guitar, and violin—in stereo.

In the courtyard pool of the RCA Building was a 53-foot Elco motor yacht, equipped to show the latest developments in marine safety and communications apparatus.

Of the RCA displays shown *above*—an animated diorama, illustrating "how radio waves are carried around the earth in a fraction of a second"; the Aviation Radio Compass; and the "Magic Switch"—the latter was particularly popular. To an audience haunted by the Lindbergh kidnapping, the "Magic Switch" had special meaning. When a spectator placed his hand near the baby doll in the bassinet, a bell rang and red lights flashed on. The protective alarm was operated by an early "electric eye."

The major theme of the Metropolitan Life Insurance Company's display was "security available to the American family," a subject that lent itself to both sculpture and murals that enlivened what could have been a potentially deadly show. In a period when a large percentage of the reading matter on a family's bookshelves might have been the handsome and practical booklets on health and diet provided without charge by the Metropolitan, this progressive company devoted much of its exhibit to the benefits it provided the community as a whole through its investments. A highlight was a model of Parkchester, its massive housing community in the Bronx then under construction and a pioneer in planned urban environments.

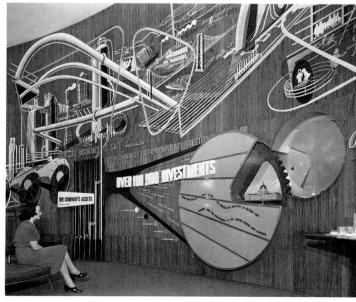

For those who became hungry while visiting the pavilions of the Communications and Business Zone, there was the Casino of Nations, one of the largest restaurants at the Fair, with a seating capacity of over 1,500. Not far from the Casino was a landmark second only to the Trylon and Perisphere —the Star Pylon. Designed by Francis Keally and Leonard Dean, the architects responsible for the Communications Building, the tower was intended to represent the force of electricity. Made of Douglas fir and rising 130 feet, the Star Pylon was fitted with tube lighting behind shields which directed light along the deeply-fluted varnished wood surface.

CHAPTER SIX

The Production and Distribution Zone

The Eastman Kodak Company Building, designed by Eugene Gerbereux, with interiors by Walter Dorwin Teague and Stowe Myers. For additional views of the building and a description of its features, see pages 74-75.

One of the major sub-themes of the Fair was the "interdependence of all peoples," and this notion was driven home with all the subtlety of a sledge hammer in the Production and Distribution Zone, particularly in its Focal Exhibit. The central point of Egmont Arens's "Three Thirds of a Nation" was right out of an elementary economics textbook: Without production there obviously would not be much distribution; and without distribution, consumption would be limited. The exhibit was divided into four sections. The first, told largely in motion pictures, was devoted to the manner in which men, science, machines, and money produce goods. The second section used dioramas, murals, and sculpture to demonstrate how the world's work was done before the industrial revolution and how machines were geared to do the job in the present. The third section used metal sculpture, shadow boxes, and graphs to dramatize the problem of equalizing the abundance produced in 1939. And the final section, using gears and mechanical symbols, contrasted "production and distribution of yesterday and today and posed the problems of tomorrow."

The *Official Guide Book* gives something of the flavor of this tediously educational exhibit: "Here an animated mural projected onto a huge cyclorama—actually a moving picture thrown on a three-dimensional screen—visualizes the vast complex of activity set in motion all over the country by every act of consumption . . . As a result of careful synchronization, you see one central action, while being aware of other actions taking place at the same time. The action of a woman powdering her nose, for example, starts off a whole series of activities involving great and small industries and an army of workers in mine, factory, warehouse, office and store, and on railroads, steamships, trucks and delivery wagons. Other equally commonplace acts of consumers arouse similar activities that are ultimately very complex."

It was all a bit much for the average 1939 woman who simply wanted to powder her nose secure in the belief that her "Lady Esther" came out of a compact and not from a rock quarry, so the Focal Exhibit, for want of an audience, folded and became, in the 1940 season, the World of Fashion, in which "the whole field of fashion is spread before you, from the basic materials to the creations of our native geniuses, including the ones who mount vegetable gardens on your hat and make you like it."

Happily, the Production and Distribution Zone contained some of the most popular pavilions in the entire Fair, and it is to these that the following pages are given.

69

MELVILLE DAVID WEINGARTEN

Above: A view, looking west from the Trylon and Perisphere, to the Production and Distribution Zone. The Court of Power, in the foreground, leads directly to four 65-foot pylons, representing the Four Elements. Beyond is the Plaza of Light and Commerce Circle, where the dome of the U.S. Steel Building and the lightning-shaped pylon of the General Electric Building are visible.

Right: The Equitable Life Assurance Company of America's "Garden of Security" provided a beautifully landscaped spot for fairgoers to rest in the shadow of John Quincy Ward's statuary group, "The Seal of Protection." The medium being the message, visitors were presumably assured and intuited the serenity that came with purchasing a life insurance policy.

Opposite page: The Carrier Corporation's igloo, designed by Reinhard & Hofmeister, was consummately silly, even in 1939, when air-conditioning was just beginning to become widespread. Still, it got its message across: Carrier meant "cool."

A UNITY OF THEME

Assessing the meaning of the Fair in July 1939, R.L. Duffus wrote, "If visual unity is lacking, there really is a unity of theme, partly deliberate, partly arising out of the very nature of our civilization and culture. When war and depression are fenced out, we seem to be moving steadily toward a splendid future. Here are many of the creative things that humanity has done. Here are evidences of what humanity wants to be and do.

"From the days of the first 'Yankee notion,' the American people have ever been lovers of gadgets. In our time the gadget, big and little, has taken on a new importance, not merely making life more convenient but tending to change our daily habits, our thoughts, our institutions. We didn't forsee that this would happen.

Now we seem to know that it has happened and will go on happening.

"Furthermore, it can be planned. The inventor has come down out of his attic and has been capitalized and incorporated. So the particular new interest of the technological and many of the purely commercial exhibits at the Fair is what the enlarged and incorporated inventor is going to do for us—and to us. We no longer think in terms of single new contrivances. We think of functions which concern us profoundly—means of getting from place to place: the automobile, the railroad, the airplane; means of transmitting information: the telephone, the radio, television; means of life and comfort: food, drink, clothing, housing, recreation."

MELVILLE DAVID WEINGARTEN

One of the largest buildings at the Fair, Pharmacy Hall was designed by Pleasants Pennington, George Lyman Paine, Jr., and I. Woodner-Silverman, with exhibits by Harvey Wiley Corbett and Donald Deskey. In 1939 the centerpiece of virtually every drugstore was the soda fountain, now gone the way of the passenger pigeon, and Pharmacy Hall presented among its many displays "The Soda Fountain of the Future," which in its sleek streamlining was remarkably like the soda fountain of 1939. There was also the inevitable "Drug Store of Tomorrow" and the "International Pharmacy," both of which sold over-the-counter drugs and sundries to fairgoers. A highlight of the exhibit was the world's largest medicine chest, with a mirror 15 feet wide and 20 feet high and shelves spacious enough to hold products the size of a human being. The medicine cabinet provided the stage for Remo Bufano's twelve-foot puppets which enacted the history of medicine, a surreal notion almost alarming to anyone in the habit of staring at himself in the medicine chest mirror the first thing on awakening. Stuyvesant Van Veen's mural on the Hall of Pharmacy was called "Pharmacy from the Beginning" and contrasted superstitious alchemy with modern scientific pharmaceutics.

The Electrical Utilities Exhibit (*right*) was designed by the firm of Harrison & Fouilhoux, creators of the Trylon and Perisphere. Behind a miniature Niagara, the fairgoer was presented with two effective illusions: "A street of 1892" and the "Avenue of Tomorrow." Entrance was by way of an ancient theater lobby, with the change from yesterday to tomorrow dramatized through old and new offices of an electric utility company, with exit provided through the waterfall via a glass-enclosed bridge (*below*).

CONRAD H. RUPPERT

MELVILLE DAVID WEINGARTEN

The main entrance of the ultra-modern Electrical Products Building, designed by A. Stewart Walker and Leon N. Gillette, was dominated by a 100-foot pylon painted a deep French blue. The chief tenant of the building (in 1939 only) was Remington Rand, whose complete line of business and home products was on display. An electric shaver, 12 feet long, with a shaving head 4 feet wide, competed in gigantism with blowups of the stubble on a man's face that showed whiskers as big as saw-logs.

THE EASTMAN KODAK COMPANY BUILDING

Photography was hardly new in 1939, but color photography, barely out of its infancy, was still a luxury just beginning to tempt an intrigued public. With sepia prints a national craze, home movie cameras dropping in price, and new film on the market, the Eastman Kodak Company moved to place itself squarely in the center of what was expected to prove a "snapshooters' fair." The company's pavilion, designed by Eugene Gerbereux, with interiors by Walter Dorwin Teague and Stowe Myers, was intended to answer all the questions of camera owners attending the Fair. Featuring a tower of enormous color blowups, with similar enlargements of Koda-chrome slides flashing on eleven mammoth screens in-side, the building was located on the well-trafficked World's Fair Boulevard, across the way from the Amuse-ment Zone. The highlight of the exhibit was the Photo-Garden, where shutterbugs could pose their families or friends against such backdrops for souvenir photo-graphs as a miniature Trylon and Perisphere.

UNITED STATES STEEL SUBSIDIARIES⸺

The New York Times thought that this remarkable building was "Martian-looking," but it resembled, perhaps unwittingly, a construction worker's hardhat. Designed by the architectural firm of York & Sawyer, with interiors by Walter Dorwin Teague and G. F. Harrell, the blue stainless-steel building was an exhibit in itself—a hemispherical dome bound together by its visible supporting girders that made it appear to be "a house built inside out." Inside were graphic displays of steel consumption, the processes of steel manufacture, gigantic graphs, and exhibits of products made from steel. On the second floor was a series of dioramas depicting the role of steel in the World of Tomorrow. At night the building was outlined with blue and white neon tubing.

THE WESTINGHOUSE BUILDING

The pavilion for the Westinghouse Electric & Manufacturing Company was designed by Skidmore & Owings and John Moss. Surrounding the "Singing Tower of Light" —an extravaganza in color, light, and sound—the Westinghouse Building was shaped like the Greek letter Omega, with two great glass-enclosed rooms forming the serifs. Ramps on either side of the court gave the fairgoer a choice of entering by way of the Hall of Electrical Living or the Hall of Electrical Power. Once inside, a bewildering array of mechanical and electrical marvels provided entertainment and education. The sheer variety could only be approximated by the *Official Guide Book:*

"Here are exhibits and demonstrations which show how man has utilized the tremendous forces of electricity. Among the wonders are a riderless bicycle that steers and balances itself; the world of the invisible, where micro-animals lead their lives; and Elektro, the Westinghouse "moto-man," a 7-foot metal man that talks, sees, smells, sings, and counts with his fingers."

MELVILLE DAVID WEINGARTEN

The contents of the 1938 Time Capsule fell into five groups: "(1) Small Articles of Common Use that we wear or use, or which contribute to our comfort, convenience, safety, or health. (2) Textiles and Materials: swatches of various types and weaves of cloth, samples of alloys, plastics, cements, asbestos, coal, etc. (3) Miscellaneous Items: seeds, books, money, type, special texts, etc. (4) An Essay in Microfilm, comprising books, speeches, excerpts from books and encyclopedias, pictures, critiques, reports, circulars, timetables and other printed or written matter—the whole producing in logical order a description of our time, our arts, sciences, techniques, sources of information and industries. A microscope is included to enable historians of the future to read the microfilm. (5) Newsreel: characteristic or significant scenes in sound film. Instructions for making a suitable projection machine to use this film are included in the microfilm Micro-File."

At the axis of the two halls of the Westinghouse Building (left), spectators peer into the "Immortal Well" for a glimpse of the Time Capsule, a record of the world of the 1930s preserved for the citizens of 6939 A.D. Beginning its 5,000-year sleep, the Time Capsule was lowered into its resting place on September 23, 1938. In the historic scene shown above, Grover Whalen (right), president of the New York World's Fair, and A. W. Robertson (left), chairman of the board of Westinghouse, watched the seven-and-a-half-foot capsule being lowered into its crypt 50 feet below the surface. (A second Westinghouse Time Capsule was buried in 1963, while the buildings of the 1964 New York World's Fair were under construction.)

As crowds ascended the electric stairway in the Hall of Power at the Westinghouse Building *(left)*, they reached a high platform above which whirled twin aluminum balls six feet in diameter. Although most spectators considered the gigantic spheres purely decorative, the device was actually a governor such as used in motors. One of the largest ever built, its construction in a public building was heralded at the time as a spectacular feat of modern engineering.

In 1940, Westinghouse turned even further in the direction of entertainment to promote science (and its products). At the *right* a throng of spectators crowds the Playground of Science, waiting their turn to help operate the Nimatron, a one-ton "electrical brain," otherwise known as a primitive computer. Other marvels included the electrical ear, the electric light which could be blown out, the stroboscope which appeared to stop the motion of whirling wheels, and the cashier's cage where an electric eye protected a stack of coins from the assault of itchy fingers. "The Battle of the Centuries" *(opposite page)* was a dishwashing contest between Mrs. Drudge, who used her hands, and Mrs. Modern, who used a 1940 Westinghouse electric dishwasher. Guess who won?

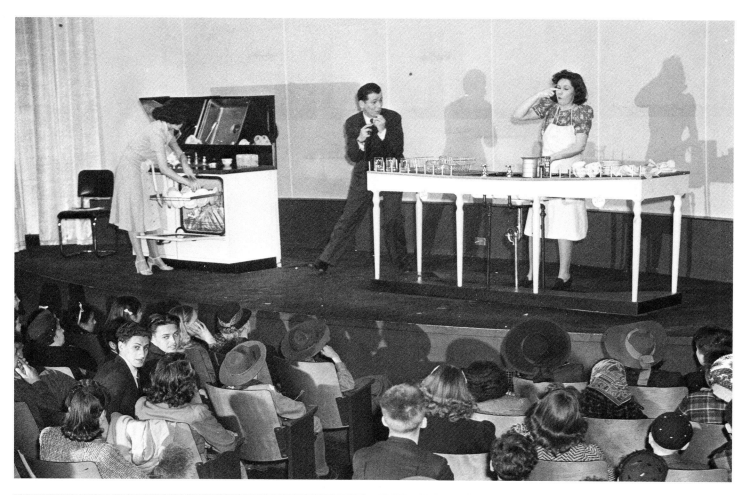

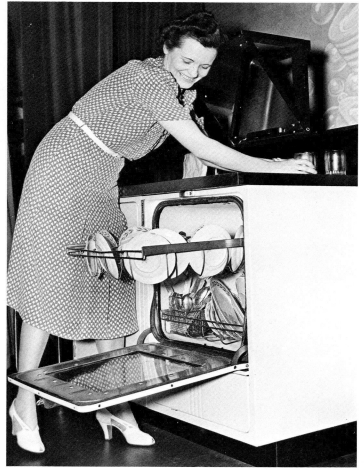

"The Bugaboo of Bugland" was "a comic movie about the microbe world" shown at Westinghouse's Playground of Science. The Technicolor film was meant to display the wonders of Westinghouse's ultraviolet Sterilamp which was trumpeted as "destroying actual microscopic animal life [i.e., germs] in one millionth of a second."

Elektro, the Westinghouse Moto-Man, was the most popular "entertainer" at the New York World's Fair. The robot was seven feet tall, weighed 260 pounds, and occasionally appeared with his "Moto-Dog," Sparko. Crowds gaped as the Robot of the Future performed feats like counting on his fingers and trading quips with his fellow performers.

THE ELGIN BUILDING⎯

At the core of the Elgin National Watch Company's ex-hibit of time-telling through the ages was the fact that correct time is determined by the stars, not by the sun. Appropriately, the company's pavilion, designed by William L. Pereira, featured a working astronomical ob-servatory which occupied half the building and allowed time readings to be made from the stars each night. There were also examples of timepieces of other ages on display, murals portraying the historical significance of time, and examples of the watchmaker's art from many countries. What fairgoers most appreciated was a booth where they could have their watches adjusted free of charge.

GENERAL ELECTRIC

Designed by the firm of Voorhees, Walker, Foley and Smith, and distinguished by a free-standing stainless-steel lightning bolt that set the tone for the exhibit, General Electric's pavilion was an unqualified crowd pleaser. In explaining how General Electric solved the problem of presenting the personality of a giant corporation for popular consumption, *Architectural Forum* offered an astute observation: "No attempt is made to cram the casual visitor with facts and figures regarding the company's multifarious activities and services; instead, he is attracted by a breathtaking and spectacular display of artificial lightning, entertained by the always-popular G. E. scientific "magic," and permitted to view—if he likes—a display of the company's products in an adjoining exhibit hall."

Of the ten million volts of artificial lightning flashing across a thirty-foot arc, *The New York Times* reported: "It's the biggest electrical charge ever demonstrated outside the laboratory, and here it is, popping off right before the visitor's eyes, with enough power to smash boulders and rive tree trunks. But General Electric also has less awesome toys in this exhibit—steel bars floating in magnetic space, talking light, disappearing phantoms, fluorescent phenomena, and a radio and television display in which visitors can take part."

Opposite page: The General Electric Building by night and by day. Because the lightning demonstration and the House of Magic shows were considered among the best at the Fair, people by the hundreds would line up to enter the exhibit at any moment of the day or night.

This page: Of the lightning demonstration in Steinmetz Hall, one observer wrote: "Astronomical figures have been commonplaces, from discussions of budget and armament costs; but ten million is still an impressive figure when applied to volts!"

In the House of Magic (*below*) anything could happen and often did. A man could walk away from his shadow, a bowl could float in air, corn could be popped by radio waves, and two chemicals could do a bubble dance. Here (*right*), without a source of heat, four lovelies fry an egg in the floating bowl.

"Harwa, an authentic Egyptian mummy" was the highlight of General Electric X-Ray Corporation's exhibit. At the *right*, the mummy and the ornate coffin lid are floodlighted for inspection by fairgoers. At the *far right*, the push of a button produces a full-length X-ray view of the skeleton within the wrappings. The mummy was borrowed for the occasion from the Egyptian Collection of Chicago's Field Museum of Natural History.

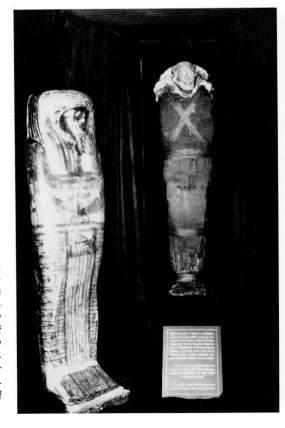

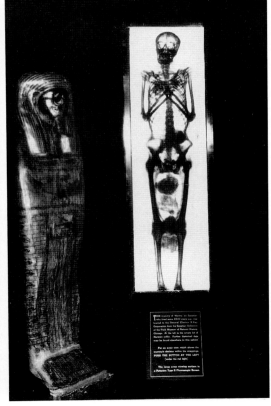

MELVILLE DAVID WEINGARTEN

GLASS INCORPORATED BUILDING

"Glass Incorporated" was the rather flat name given the three companies responsible for the construction of one of the loveliest buildings at the Fair—Corning Glass Works, Owens-Illinois Glass Company, and the Pittsburgh Plate Glass Company. (In 1940 as the Fair became less self-consciously educational, the building was simply called "The Glass Center.") Designed by Shreve, Lamb and Harmon, the architects of the Empire State Building, and with exhibits by Skidmore & Owings, the structure was one of the most frequently photographed pavilions. Built almost entirely of glass block, plate glass, and structural glass, it had a gleaming 107-foot tower of glass block set off by blue plate-glass fins. The tower was illuminated from within, and a metal spiral, outlined by neon tubing, made it an outstanding Fair landmark, especially at night.

Chief among the exhibits was an enormous glass furnace at which glass blowers demonstrated their art; a three-room furnished suite, where even the curtains and upholstery were made of glass; looms that spun glass into fiberglass fabrics; the largest piece of clear crystal ever cast, Sidney Waugh's statue of "Atlantica"; a miniature bottle plant in full operation; and, for the sheer fun of it, a collection of distorting funhouse mirrors that never failed to draw the largest crowds.

THE PETROLEUM INDUSTRY EXHIBITION

One of the largest oil derricks in the world, in actual operation, made the Petroleum Industry Exhibition a popular landmark on the fairgrounds. Veteran "roughnecks," brought to the Fair from the great oil fields of the Southwest, manned the derrick in a continuous drilling operation.

The building, designed by Voorhees, Walker, Foley and Smith, with displays by Gilbert Rohde, was in the form of an equilateral triangle 80 feet high, resting on four huge aluminum painted oil tanks. Its walls rose in four flaring tiers painted in graduated shades of blue. Lighted at night by concealed fluorescent tubes, the building soon became a favorite subject for camera buffs.

Inside the building, the four "support tanks" housed separate exhibits: "Petroleum in Transportation," "Petroleum in Industry," "Petroleum in the House and on the Farm," and "Petroleum and Your Pocketbook." In the great center hall, an animated color film, "Pete Roleum and His Cousins," directed by the young Joseph Losey, was projected on a mammoth hanging screen.

Four large murals by William T. Schwarz decorated the inner walls of the Petroleum Industry Exhibition's Great Hall of Industry. Each mural depicted one phase in the story of petroleum—*Production, Transportation, Research,* and *Refining.* Shown on these pages are *Refining* and *Research.*

THE CONSOLIDATED EDISON BUILDING——

A 9,000 foot wall of water provided the Consolidated Edison Building with a unique exterior. By day this 42 foot wall of water was crystal white. By night it became an iridescent colonnade of sparkling blue water, before which fountain jets simulated the action of ballet dancers. The constantly changing fountain display, called the "Water Ballet," was the work of sculptor Alexander Calder; the building, the work of Harrison & Fouilhoux.

The fairgoer who ever dreamed of seeing the whole New York panorama, from Coney Island to Westchester, could see it at the Con Ed Building. "The City of Light," a diorama long as a city block and high as a three-story building, formed the central exhibit. It was complete with Manhattan's towers and subways in action, and it was dramatized with sound effects—including a thunderstorm—and lighting to simulate a twenty-four hour cycle in the city's life. It was immensely popular.

Sunset (*left*) and night (*below*) come to "The City of Light," Consolidated Edison's block-long diorama. Thousands of electric lights provided a constantly changing spectacle, with dawn, midday, afternoon, twilight, and night effects following one another in each twelve-minute performance.

Building the diorama (*below, left*) was an exercise in skill and precision. The section shown features the Empire State Building—102 stories—which in miniature stood twenty-two feet high.

Opposite page: A side wall of the Metals Building, showing a portion of André Duranceau's mural of Hercules, god of strength and power. At the bottom of the page are illustrated three of the many dioramas displayed by the Yale and Towne Manufacturing Company to depict the history of lock-making from the devices of the ancient Egyptians to the modern pin tumbler lock invented by Linus Yale.

This page: A display of locomotive bearings in the Timken Roller Bearing Company exhibit; an enlarged model of the copper atom in the Copper and Brass Industry exhibit; and the exhibit of the American Chain & Cable Company.

THE METALS BUILDING

On the exterior walls of the Metals Building, designed by William Gehron, Benjamin W. Morris, and Robert B. O'Connor, were four large murals by André Duranceau, portraying Hercules, god of strength and power; Vulcan, god of fire; Neptune, god of water; and Aeolus, god of air. Although it was a long way from the mythology of ancient Greece to the mastery of modern metallurgy, the gap was bridged in this industrial exhibit by showing how modern industry harnessed the ancient arts to contemporary uses.

The Metals Building displayed the manufacture of steel cable, of wire rope, of chains, the modern processes of converting ore into metal and metal into industrial machines and structures. A dozen major companies participated and exhbited mechanical conveying equipment, furnaces and rolling mills, elevators, bridges, and roller bearings. In short, copper, brass, and allied materials were exhibited from mine to finished product.

THE DU PONT BUILDING

Designed by Walter Dorwin Teague, R. J. Harper, and A. M. Erickson, the "Wonder World of Chemistry" pavilion built for the E. I. du Pont de Nemours & Company, Inc., featured a spectacular 105-foot tower, representing the complex apparatus used in chemical laboratories. The tower was surrounded by a steel framework, seventy feet high, symbolic of the walkways found in chemical plants. Inside, in the Hall of Chemistry, were shown some of the laboratory and research processes that made the chemical wonders of 1939 possible, as well as the actual production of such things as plastics and synthetic fabric fibers. (Nylon stockings were one of the sensations of the 1940 Fair, just as du Pont's cellophane had been one of the chief novelties at 1933's Century of Progress Exhibition.) At night, changing lights within the Tower of Chemistry simulated the bubbling of chemical liquids.

In the research section of the du Pont exhibit (*left*) were demonstrated some of the ways by which the chemist was constantly deconstituting nature's raw materials and recombining them in new ways and forms better suited to modern needs. (Nylon, for example, was made basically from coal, water, and air.)

In another part of the building—in a separate hall where in 1939 the Tutterman Marionettes showed how chemistry affects modern life, and in 1940 the colorful variety of crystal formations were made visible by polarized light—Miss Chemistry held court (*above*). Clothed from the tip of her shoes to the top of her head in products created by chemistry, Miss Chemistry (known as Miss 1940 a year later) was a veritable fashion plate of synthetics.

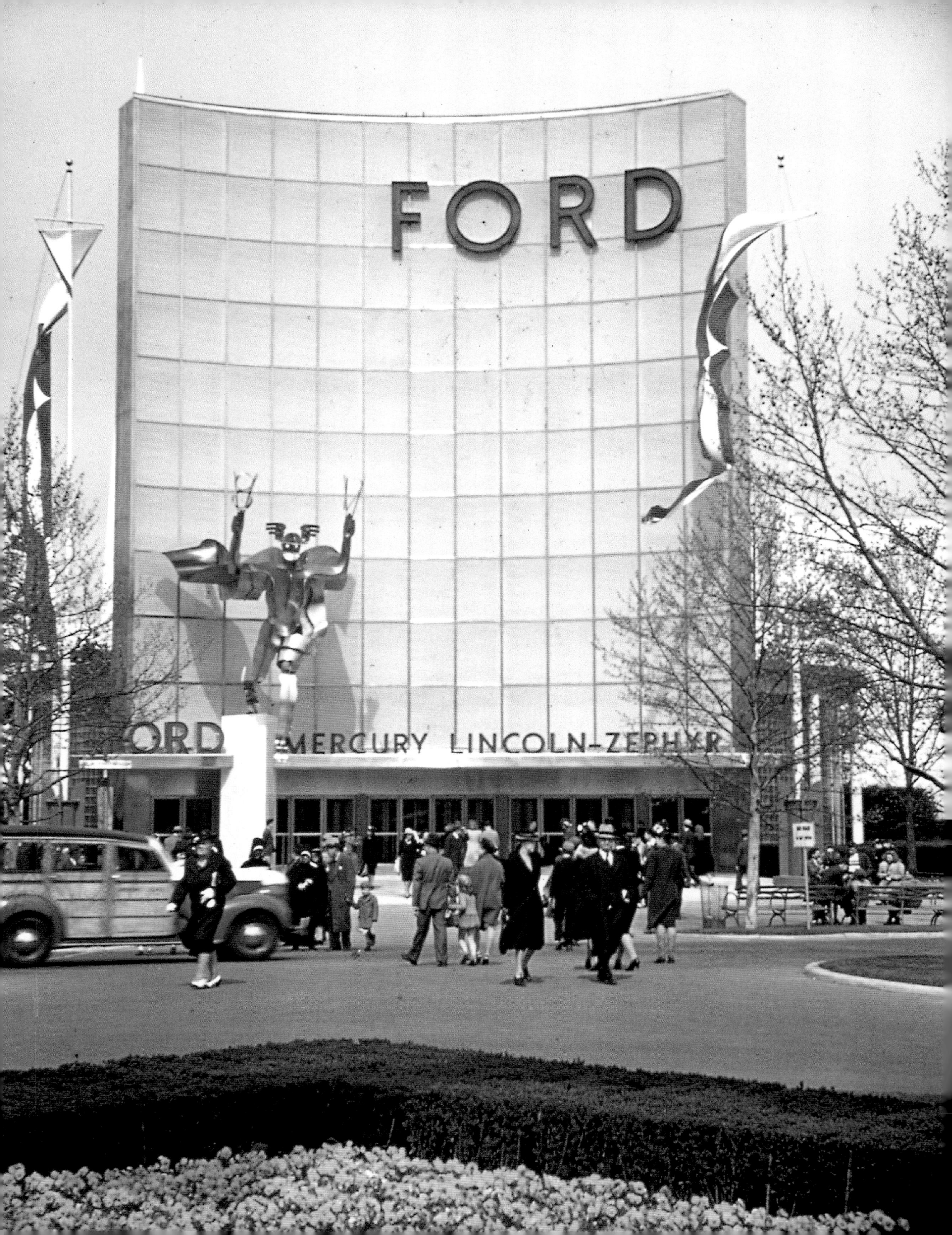
FORD
ORD MERCURY LINCOLN-ZEPHYR

CHAPTER SEVEN

The Transportation Zone

The imposing Entrance Hall of the Ford Motor Company Building, the façade of which was completely rebuilt in glass for the 1940 season, was only one of four components that made up the massive pavilion known as the Ford Exposition. Designed by Albert Kahn, whose many buildings for Ford are in themselves a major chapter of American architectural history, the Ford Exposition was one of the most popular attractions of the Fair. Other views of the Ford exhibit are pictured on pages 116 through 121.

Norman Bel Geddes, creator of the Futurama, said it best: "Today, speed is the cry of our era." Although the economy was at a standstill, speed was the passion of the 1930s. No one quite knew where he was going, why he was going, or what he would find when he got there, but in Depression America it was important to get there quickly. Most dreamed of going by car. (Will Rogers remarked that America was the first nation in the history of the world to go to the poorhouse in an automobile.) While railroads were in the last gasp of their greatness in the United States, and aviation was just beginning to come into its own, cars were the very essence of the American dream of mobility and escape, and highways the most direct route to the World of Tomorrow. For this reason, the Transportation Zone was dominated by automobile pavilions. While railroads, aviation, and marine transportation each had a single Fair building, automobiles had no less than three. And, though no one seemed to notice at the time, the major theme of the most popular attraction of the Fair—General Motors' Futurama—was that America was going to have to be completely remade in the image of the automobile if it were to reap the benefits of the World of Tomorrow. A vast network of highways was going to change our lives for the better, Bel Geddes predicted. He was half right.

The general tone of the Transportation Zone was, like the decade of the thirties itself, peculiarly Janus-like. It looked back in time in order to see the future. The Ford Exhibition, *Railroads on Parade,* the Focal Exhibit—all explored where America had been in order to see where she was going.

The Focal Exhibit, located in the Chrysler Building, depicted the story of transportation from prehistoric times and emphasized the fact that the world had steadily grown smaller, its people drawn closer together by improved means of transportation. In designing the exhibit, Donald Deskey sought to show the story of man's progress from the footpath to the stratosphere. History was dramatized by a huge map with flashing lights which charted the changes in man's speed, from the days of sandal-clad runners through the time of galley ships, camels, chariots, covered wagons, the pony express, and the clipper ship. Finally, the railroad, the steamship, the automobile, and the airplane showed how in 1939 man could circle the globe in a few days. The visionary climax was a rocket blasting passengers into space, but Fairgoers only had to cross the street—to General Motors' aptly named "Highways and Horizons" exhibit—to know that America's future lay with the automobile. Rocketships would have to wait until a later world of tomorrow.

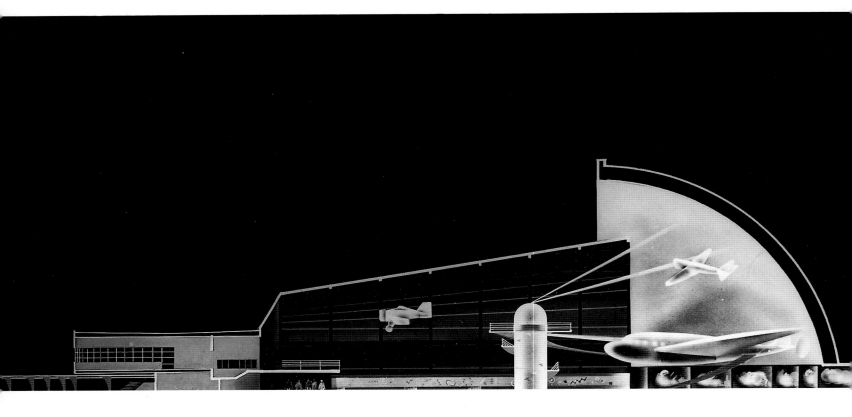

The Aviation Building (*opposite page*) was designed by William Lescaze and J. Gordon Carr to resemble an airplane hangar embodying the architects' idea of "flight in space," but wags persisted in likening the pavilion to a dirigible nosing its way into a park band shell. While the building did in fact resemble a highly streamlined version of actual airports of the 1930s—an office-waiting room attached to a hangar—one element, though admittedly dramatic, defied an even rudimentary understanding of how a hangar operated: four transport planes were suspended from the hangar ceiling at an angle which made them appear to be coming in for a landing—and the certain destruction of the waiting room.

Surreal in its impact, dramatic in its beauty, the Marine Transportation Building was designed by Ely Jacques Kahn and Muschenheim & Brounn. Eighty-foot prows of gigantic superliners towered at each side of the entrance and seemed to slice through the building itself. Visitors entered the marine exhibit on a gangplank slung between the enormous prows. Within, the National Council of American Shipbuilders presented a complete display of the past, present, and future of shipping.

CONRAD H. RUPPERT

Stretching along the Court of Railways for nearly a quarter of a mile, the Railroad Building (*right*), designed by Eggers and Higgins, was the largest structure in the Fair. Five murals by Griffith Baily Coale embellished its eight-story exterior.

The industrial designer Raymond Loewy, who was consulting designer for the entire Railroads display, is pictured, *above*, aboard his 526-ton steam locomotive, the 6100, the largest ever built for the Pennsylvania Railroad. A close-up of the 6100's wheels, which ran continuously on a roller bed at sixty miles an hour, is seen, *opposite*, with one of the many locomotives on display in the huge train yards, Henry Dreyfuss's Hudson-type engine for the New York Central.

MELVILLE DAVID WEINGARTEN

MELVILLE DAVID WEINGARTEN

RAILROADS

The old and the new of railroading met in the gigantic Court of Railways, a sixteen-acre display of locomotives, trains, and the men who made them run. Twenty-seven principal railroads east of the Mississippi participated, and there were three and a half miles of track and enough special exhibits to take a railroad buff a week to cover. In the yards stood the British-built John Bull locomotive of 1831 alongside a modern 140-foot Pennsylvania streamlined giant that ran continuously at sixty miles an hour on a roller bed. Nearby were dozens of other trains from every period. The highlight of the exhibit was *Railroads on Parade,* a panoramic musical drama performed by a cast of 250 on an outdoor stage.

NEW YORK
WORLD'S FAI
1939

Railroads on Parade was a pageant about the "romance of transport" from covered wagon days to the streamlined trains of 1939. Created and directed by Edward Hungerford, it aimed to highlight the role transportation played in the opening and development of the vast American continent. The spectacle was presented on an outdoor stage, 250 feet wide by 100 feet deep, that provided standard gauge tracks for the "parade" of historic and modern trains, broad highways for vehicular traffic, a performing stage for a cast of 250 actors and actresses, and a channel in the rear for a review of early watercraft. The amphitheater for viewing the show seated 4,000. Admission was only twenty-five cents. Music was by Kurt Weill. The mural-style cover for the souvenir program was rendered by William A. Mackay in 1938.

RAILROADS·ON·PARADE

"*Railroads on Parade* records the magnificent progress of rail transport in America for the past 110 years. It begins with the first efforts of men who, inspired with bold vision and foresight, worked to achieve the unification of a continent, and it leads to a glowing picture of railroad operation in the United States of 1939. To fashion this picture so that it may tell its story briefly had been the aim and ambition of its creator. The effort has been to condense, to epitomize, by a series of stage pictures, with adequate narration and incidental music, to create a sharp impression of this outstanding example of man's achievement in America . . . Into every corner of our social and economic existence, the railroad is tightly interwoven. It is the backbone of the country . . . its veritable lifeblood . . . If it were to die, then the nation would die."—*from the souvenir program for* Railroads on Parade.

Railroads on Parade opened in Quincy, Massachusetts, in 1826 with the oxen-drawn "Gridley Bryant" hauling stones on Bunker Hill on the Granite Railroad, progressed to the historic joining of East and West with the legendary golden spike, moved on to the famous "999" which set a world's record in 1893, and ended with the streamlined luxury travel of 1939. The scenes shown here illustrate the Brobdingnagian outdoor stage and the elaborate costumes and sets by Harry Horner.

CONRAD H. RUPPERT

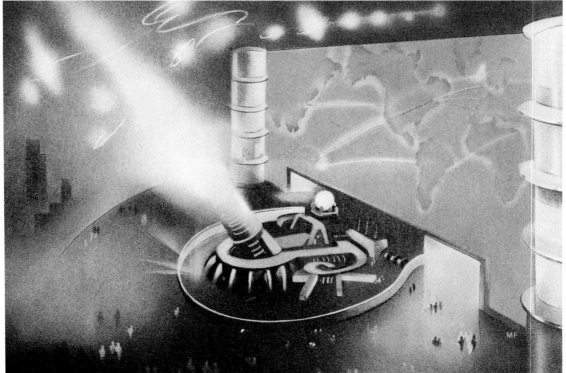

The Chrysler Motor Company Building (*opposite page*), designed by James Gambrel Rogers, featured displays by Donald Deskey, at the center of which was a series of "illusion boxes"—a combination of large dioramas, lights, and mirrors—that showed such historical figures as Lady Godiva, George Washington, and Buffalo Bill trading in their ancient means of transportation for shiny, new Chryslers. Something of a yawn even by 1939 standards, the show itself was traded in in 1940 for the first Technicolor three-dimensional movie ever made. Wearing Polaroid glasses to perceive the 3-D effect, audiences were treated to a musical starring animated car parts that danced and sang. Among the other exhibits was "the Amazing Talking Plymouth."

Also within the Chrysler Building was the Transportation Zone's Focal Exhibit, a mixed-media history of transportation, designed by Donald Deskey. The climax of the exhibit was the departure of a rocketship from a Rocketport of the future (*opposite page*). "Here," as *The New York Times* reported, "with startling effects of light, speed, sound, and distance, a rocketship is loaded into a gigantic gun and launched into the night, to go winging into the vast reaches of the sky toward London." One wonders whether Deskey had been influenced by *Things to Come,* the 1936 English science-fiction film in which rockets, like Puffed Wheat, are shot from guns.

Designed by William Berle Thompson with Wilbur Watson & Associates, the B.F. Goodrich Company Building (*right*) consisted of two wings that curved away from its main entrance to create an egg-shaped field. The purpose of the field was to showcase the daredevil stunt driving performances of Jimmie Lynch and his troupe. And the purpose of the racing drivers was both to draw crowds and to demonstrate the indestructability of Goodrich tires. Among the other displays were an automobile suspended in midair by a strip of rubber, miniature tires created for fairgoers while they waited, free instruction in safe driving for those who were inclined to learn, and the "Tire Guillotine," an enormous sharpened blade that would never fail to come a cropper when up against a Goodrich product. In 1940, also a good year for "all-girl" orchestras, Jimmie Lynch added "two pretty 'She-Devils'" to his hell-raising troupe.

THE GENERAL MOTORS BUILDING

General Motors' "Highways and Horizons" exhibit occupied a seven-acre site on the Avenue of Transportation. Designed by Albert Kahn, Inc., the General Motors Building, where the many displays were housed, was actually four buildings centered around an open-air cross-street, a full-scale street intersection of 1960 that played a significant part in Norman Bel Geddes's Futurama. The most popular exhibit of the Fair, the Futurama attracted large crowds throughout the 1939-1940 seasons.

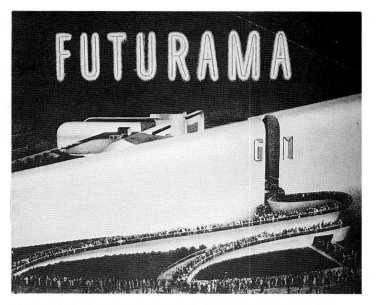

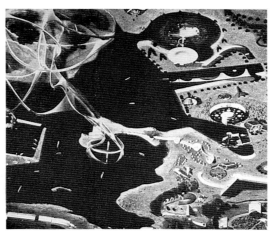

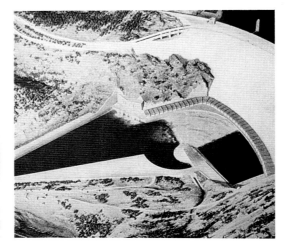

Once the visitor to the Futurama took his seat, he was whisked high above the world of 1960, where he saw and heard the following:

"Directly ahead [*far left*] is a modern experimental farm and dairy. Note the terraced fields and strip planting. The fruit trees bear abundantly under individual glass housings. Here is an aeration plant purifying the lake water and distributing it hundreds of miles throughout the countryside."

"Now we aproach a modern university center. Here, in buildings of simple but functional architecture, the youth of 1960 study for their future in a world of still greater progress and achievement."

"Looming ahead is a 1960 Motorway intersection. By means of ramped loops, cars may make right and left turns at rates of speed up to 50 miles per hour. The turning-off lanes are elevated and depressed. There is no interference from the straight ahead traffic in the higher speed lanes."

"Night falls on the countryside. But, what's this just ahead? An amusement park in full swing. A merry-go-round— a ferris wheel—boys and girls shrieking with glee on a pretzel-like sky-ride. Here's fun and merriment in this world of tomorrow."

"Just as improved highways have benefited the farmer, so have they added to the comforts of living and economic welfare of those in industrial communities. Here is a prosperous and thriving steel town. . . ."

"Now we are traveling high above the mountains and valleys below—a bird's-eye view of a paradise for vacationers. With the fast highways of 1960, the slogan 'See America First' has taken on new meaning and importance."

"Contrast the straight, unobstructed path of the Motorway at the right with that of the twisting, winding, ordinary road to the left of the quiet and peaceful monastery. One marvels at the complete accord of this man-made highway with the breath-taking scenic beauty of its route."

"Just beyond is a miracle in engineering—a giant mountain lake dam with its spillway, companion buildings, and hydro-electric power plants, providing service for hundreds of miles around. The various speed lanes of the Motorway converge on one end of this dam and continue their route across the top of it."

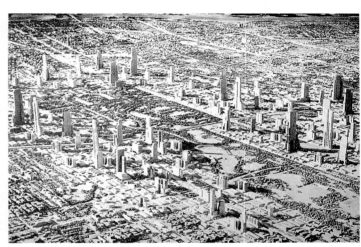

The journey across the America of 1960 continued with a descent from the mountains on "the various lanes of the Motorway" towards a towering city, forty miles away. The traveler then came across "a close-up view of a great suspension bridge, forming the motor-traffic gateway to the city." As he approached the city, the visitor was banked "high over it for a spectacular view of its many wonders." Then he saw it—"the city of 1960, with its abundant sunshine, fresh air, fine green parkways—all the result of thoughtful planning and design." And then he saw the city again—in close-up. Finally, he saw an important intersection in the great metropolis of 1960—and the Futurama ride was over.

Then came the "hook." "Ladies and gentlemen, in a moment we will arrive actually on this very street intersection—to become a part of the World of Tomorrow." And they did. "And now in each of the four buildings on this street intersection of the future, General Motors invites you to visit its many interesting and exciting displays and exhibits. See the thrilling science stage show in the Auditorium—see the beautiful motor car display—the Diesel, Frigidaire, Fisher Body, and Overseas exhibits."

It was all brilliantly conceived—a magnificently entertaining journey into the future by hundreds of thousands of consumers—only to be dropped off onto a "1960" stage set filled with the gleaming, streamlined products of 1939 just waiting to be bought.

As they passed by the extraordinary scale models that contributed to the illusion of flying over the world of 1960, passengers aboard the Futurama traveled in their "carry-go-round" chairs through about a third of a mile in and about on several levels of the General Motors Building. The moving conveyor carried 552 sound-chairs. Its capacity was about 2,150 persons per hour, or a total of approximately 28,000 persons per day. With the aid of aerial photographs and maps of many sections of the United States, the Futurama was created from 408 separate sections made by hundreds of skilled artists and craftsmen working under the direction of Norman Bel Geddes, designer, and with George Wittbold, builder. The illusion of distance, suggested by the scale of models, is evident in the photographs shown here. A workman carries a large model of a building used in a close-up scene, while Bel Geddes himself is pictured with the miniature models used for a bird's-eye scene.

Clockwise from top: Among the many exhibits within the General Motors Buildings were a handsome spiral-ramped hall of copper, glass, and rosewood in which the latest Chevrolet, Pontiac, Oldsmobile, Buick, LaSalle, and Cadillac models were shown; a revolving display for Quaker spark plugs; a demonstration of the "Talking Flashlight," showing how speech can be transmitted over a light beam; and Fisher Body's full-size "X-ray car," constructed of plexiglas, then a newly developed transparent plastic.

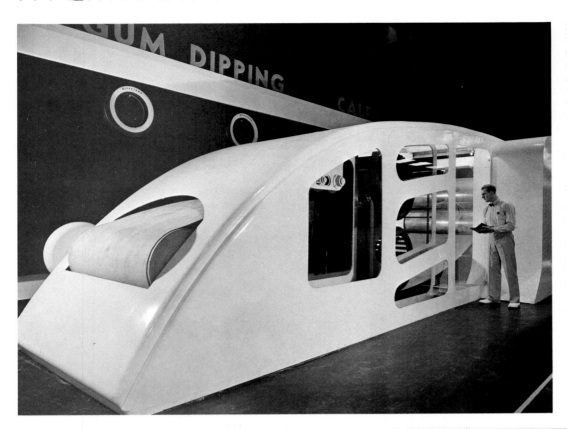

Surmounted by a long vertical fin 100 feet high, the Firestone Tire & Rubber Company Building (*opposite*) was designed by Wilbur Watson and Associates. The L-shaped building featured a rotunda entrance at the intersection of the two wings. The tone of the Firestone display is humorously captured in a *New York Times* report: "Not content with a modern tire factory that turns out a finished automobile tire every four minutes [*this page*], the exhibit also includes a farm complete with house, barns, pigs, and chickens [*opposite*]. For rubber has gone rural. All the farm vehicles are equipped with rubber tires, and one half expects to see the chickens in rubber boots—but they aren't. The tire factory is equipped with a battery of streamlined, chromium-finished machines and shows the whole process, from crude rubber to tire ready to go on a wheel."

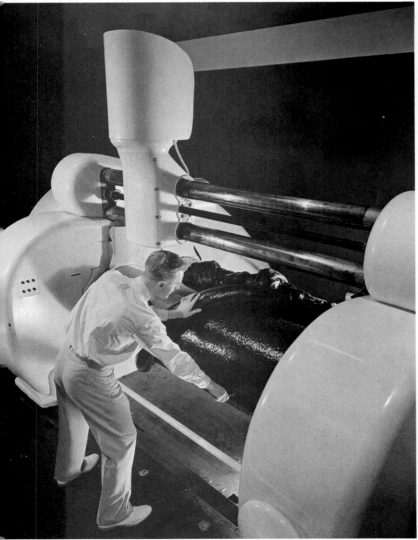

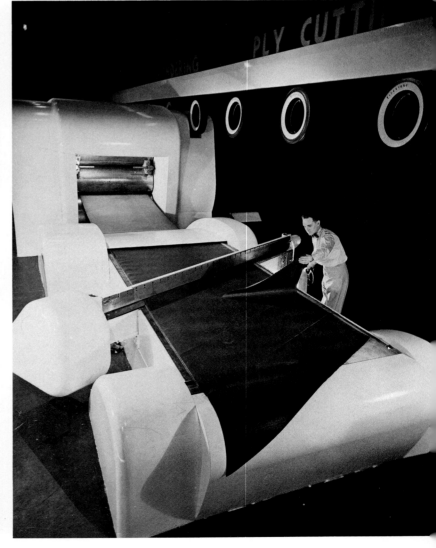

THE FORD MOTOR COMPANY BUILDING——

Ignoring for the moment the company's interior displays, which several architectural critics considered the best in the Fair, the exterior of the Ford Motor Company's pavilion, known as "the Ford Exposition," was highly regarded for its functional beauty. Adorned with a free-floating stainless-steel sculpture of Mercury by Robert Foster that appeared at the building's crown in 1939 and above the newly designed entrance façade in 1940 (*opposite*), the building was outwardly dominated by its half-mile spiral ramp ("the Road of Tomorrow") on which visitors road-tested Fords, Mercurys, and Lincoln-Zephyrs. The building also featured a generous interior court in which visitors could relax and enjoy picnic lunches amid pleasantly landscaped surroundings. Designed by Albert Kahn, Inc., the pavilion was lavishly furnished with ultra-modern fittings by Walter Dorwin Teague.

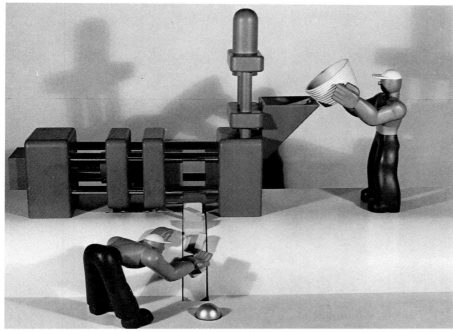

The heart of the Ford display was the deservedly popular "Ford Cycle of Production," designed by Walter Dorwin Teague. One hundred feet in diameter at the base, 30 feet high, and weighing 152 tons, the base of the Cycle revolved slowly in a circular moat and carried 87 amusing animated models by Peter Haller that illustrated every stage in the production of a Ford automobile from mine and field to the finished product.

Uniting the pistons and valves of an automobile with a pictorial representation of how industry harnesses the energy of the sun, Henry Billings created a great animated mural (*opposite, below*) that was considered in its time "an altarpiece of science." Seventy feet long and 30 feet high, the mural was on display in the pavilion's vast entrance hall, its moving parts synchronized to work exactly as they did in the engine of a Ford.

All through the 1930s, ballet—once the exclusive preserve of high-hats—was becoming popularized. Rodgers' and Hart's *On Your Toes* was a 1936 Broadway success and a 1939 film; Fred Astaire played a Russian ballet dancer in 1937's *Shall We Dance*; *The Goldwyn Follies* included both classical and modern ballet in 1938; and, of course, Harriet Hoctor, a dancer best known for her uncanny ability to kick herself in the back of her head *en pointe*, flitted in and out of several Hollywood films of the Depression. It was inevitable, then, for popular ballet to make an appearance at the 1940 Fair. *A Thousand Times Neigh,* an original comic ballet, featured members of American Ballet Caravan and was performed twelve times a day at the brand-new Ford Playhouse. In it, Dobbin, played by two dancers, was challenged by the horseless carriage and learned over the years that retirement wasn't so bad after all.

CHAPTER EIGHT

The Food Zone

Designed by Skidmore & Owings with John Moss, the Wonder Bakery was created for the Continental Baking Company, makers of "slo-baked" Wonder Bread. The graceful white facade was dotted with red, blue, and yellow balloons, suggestive of the bread's colorful wrapper.

Fifty years after the event, the notion of an entire area of the New York World's Fair devoted solely to food might conjure up an image of succulent gourmet foods from around the globe, the latest in expensive cookware and kitchen gadgets, and renowned chefs offering instruction in how to use to culinary advantage a pinch of some exotic herb or spice. But the world was a far, far different place in the 1930s, when Franklin D. Roosevelt was able to see "one-third of a nation ill-housed, ill-clad, ill-fed." Sound nutrition for good health was an issue of importance during the Depression. At a time when large numbers of adults suffered from rotting teeth and children were disfigured by scurvy or rickets, Americans needed to learn the basics of the new science of nutrition.

The Focal Exhibit of the Food Zone was therefore educational with a vengeance, but it overcame the potential dullness of its good intentions through the genius of its designer, Russel Wright. Much taken with the surrealism exhibit at the Museum of Modern Art in 1936, he created an animated display that would have done both Salvador Dali and Carlton Fredericks proud. As *The New York Times* reported, "The surrealists have turned potatoes, piecrust, and fat green peppers to strange artistic purposes, but this focal exhibit in Food Building No. 3 is probably the first instance of surrealism being taken into camp by the dietitians. Russel Wright has thoroughly enjoyed himself, and once the visitor catches the spirit of the proceedings, he, too, will be amused by silk-lined potatoes, fur-covered eggs, and velvet pot roasts. The idea is to dramatize food and food properties in an entertaining way. The climactic display is a panorama with such objects as an avocado bearing five jewels, a flock of lobsters flying merrily over the hills, an eye blinking accusingly from a cave, a clock inside a tin can with its hands racing backward, and an aqueduct pouring roses into a desert. A recorded voice explains all. The jewels in the avocado represent carbohydrates, fats, minerals, proteins, and vitamins. The flying lobsters are seafood in transit. The eye is man seeing at night with the help of vitamin A. The clock means that canned foods bring harvest season to the consumer at any time in the year."

The entire exhibit was a witty way of getting across the notion of basic food groups and balanced diets to the general public, and it was a needed relief from the standard hawking of commercial products in other pavilions of the zone. In 1940, with the war on, idealism shattered, and the Fair an almost certain financial failure, the nutrition-minded Food Building No. 3 became the Coca-Cola pavilion.

Publicists for Swift & Company claimed that the famous meat packager's pavilion resembed a good-old American hot dog, while the *Official Guide Book* likened the building to "a gleaming super-airliner." But Skidmore & Owings' Swift Building looked very much like a streamlined ark with a crew of hams and sausages aboard. In fact, hams and sausages were what the display was all about, and, when a fairgoer completed his tour of dioramas showing how a hog becomes a ham, he could gaze through the glass-enclosed smokehouse, where the three little pigs, times a hundred, were being cured. In addition there was a frankfurter factory in operation that turned out the "official red-hots" of the Fair. *The New York Times* hinted that the display was somewhat wearying, but begrudgingly allowed that its highlight was "the fragrance of smoking ham."

"The Heinz pickle has been a souvenir at almost every fair since 1893, a kind of perennial fair personality," wrote *The New York Times*. "Here it is again, in an ultra-modern setting dominated by a sixty-five-foot column supporting a figure of the Goddess of Perfection." The H. J. Heinz Company Dome was the creation of Leonard M. Schultze and Archibald Brown, with exterior murals by Domenico Mortellito. The sculpture, which in 1940 was moved outside to the top of the dome, was by Raymond Barger. In addition to free samples of the company's 57 varieties, an animated stage show dramatized "the story of strained baby food," and a six-foot "Mr. Aristocrat Tomato Man," in top hat and tails, sang, nodded his tomato head, and smacked his lips.

With the possible exception of Charlie McCarthy, who was the unchallenged star of the Standard Brands Building, almost everything else in the exhibit suffered from terminal gigantism, including the "World's Largest Store Counter," one section of which is shown *above*. Of a display of mammoth vitamins, one writer asked: "Ever see a vitamin? Here they are, all five types of them, big enough to scare one out of a year's growth if seen coming down a back road on a moonless night."

Half the kids brought up on Junket rennet-custards in the thirties and forties recall the gustatory experience as very much like eating colored chalk, but the other half thrived on it, preferring its smooth texture to lumpy puddings. "The 'Junket' Folks," a display for Chas. Hansen's Laboratory, Inc., in the Food Building (North), featured attendants in Danish peasant garb who demonstrated just how easy it was to make the yummy dessert. In 1940, "Miss Junket" greeted "children of all ages" and escorted them "to the counter to be served with delicious rennet-custards."

The mural by Carlo Ciampaglia over the entrance to the Food Building (North) represented the production, consumption, and distribution of food. The principal panel has as its main theme a single figure, personifying nature. On the left side is the story of production and harvesting. On the right is shown the consumption of food. The mural was 26 feet high and 76 feet wide.

Designed by Voorhees, Walker, Foley and Smith to show "the actual operation of getting clean milk from clean cows, and what happens to it afterwards," the Borden Company Building centered around a Walker-Gordon "rotolactor," or rotating mechanical milking platform. The public area surrounding the rotolactor was entirely open to the outside and arranged in a series of steps, giving four rows of spectators a clear view of the milking operation. Following the clockwise rotation of the platform (which necessitated special training for cows accustomed to being milked on their right side), fairgoers moved to the processing and bottling exhibits. The entire show was a great crowd-pleaser. (In 1940, an element of kitsch was added with "Elsie the Borden Cow's Boudoir.")

Little fat "Wonder Bakers" and characters from *Alice in Wonderland* decorated the entrance of Skidmore & Owings' building for the Continental Baking Company, a decorative theme repeated in murals inside. A gaggle of Alices beckoned the fairgoer to the "Bakery Wonderland," a model bakery with all kinds of machines in operation, turning out Wonder Bread and Hostess Cupcakes, a good share of which supplied the Wonder Sandwich Bar located at the side of the building. Located at the rear of the building was one of the most unusual features of the Fair—a wheat field. The grain was purportedly the first wheat grown in New York City since 1871.

The circus came to town in the Beech-Nut Packing Company Building. The ingeniously animated entertainment, billed as the "Biggest Little Show on Earth," featured more than five hundred "performers"—acrobats, aerialists, animals, and clowns—all of which drew vast crowds. The Beech-Nut pavilion, designed by Magill Smith, also featured dioramas on the cultivation of coffee beans and free samples of the company's products.

Within the Food Building (South), the little Sunshine bakers (*left*) that had appeared for years in Loose-Wiles Biscuit Comany advertisements put on a show to sing the praises of Sunshine's Krispy Crackers. The Sealtest Building (*below*), designed by DeWitt Clinton Pond, was distinguished by three towering fins bearing the names of Kraft and Sheffield, two prominent members of the National Dairy Products Company family. Within the building was a milk pasteurization and bottling plant large enough to serve a town of 15,000, and a variety of other dairy-inspired exhibits, including a modernistic "dairy fountain luncheonette."

The Schaefer Center, designed by the firm of Eggers & Higgins, was a popular-priced restaurant seating 1,600 people and featuring the Fair's largest open-air bar. Among the foods prepared in the restaurant was a variety of dishes made with beer as an ingredient. A mural over the 120-foot bar, depicting the history of Schaefer Beer, "America's oldest lager beer," was the work of Arthur Crisp.

Every effort seemed to be made to protect the public from the Distilled Spirits Exhibit, Inc. Although Prohibition had ended at the start of 1933, the liquor industry couched everything about its display in tones of abject apology. Designed by Morris Sanders, the building (as the *Official Guide Book* was quick to point out) was the only *American* pavilion to feature distilled spirits. Even the publicist who wrote the original caption for the photograph shown here had to emphasize that only *water* was flowing from the fountain in the foreground.

While fairgoers couldn't actually eat tobacco, the weed was everywhere apparent in the Food Zone, perhaps because it was supposedly "toasted." The American Tobacco Company Building, designed by the firm of Francisco and Jacobus, was shaped like a carton of Luck Strike "Greens," which, in fact, could be purchased within and mailed to friends as a souvenir of the Fair (see page 211). Within the building were cigarette-making machines and other displays on the making and marketing of "Luckies."

The General Cigar Company Building, designed by Ely Jacques Kahn, was not for the ladies. Although visitors undoubtedly peeked at the demonstrations of how White Owl cigars were made, most male fairgoers dropped in to check the two electric scoreboards that followed, inning by inning, the major league baseball games. (In 1940, the pavilion was renamed the White Owl Building and broadcast the latest war news as well as the ball scores.)

WORKS PROGRESS ADMINISTRA

CHAPTER NINE

The Community Interests Zone

Designed by Delano & Aldrich, the Works Progress Administration Building was created to showcase the achievements of the WPA in providing jobs for more than three million unemployed workers, thus adding to the nation's permanent wealth. In an interior setting devised and built by its own membership, the exhibit included murals, sculpture, architectural models, crafts, and other works by WPA artists. A theater offered motion pictures and puppet shows created by members. Philip Guston's mural, "Work—The American Way," was above the main entrance. In 1940 the name of the pavilion was changed to the Federal Works Agency Building.

There was a lot of high-minded talk about what the Community Interests Zone was supposed to be about, but nobody seemed to know for sure. Was it intended to suggest service in the nation's interest, as the inclusion of the Works Progress Administration Building would imply? Or was it meant to embody the motto "In God We Trust," as the presence of the Temple of Religion would testify? If so, what was "Gas Wonderland" doing there, and why wasn't it together with the Electric Utilities Exhibit in the Production and Distribution Zone? The fact is that the Community Interests Zone was like a rarely used guest bedroom: It was a convenient place to stash the things that just didn't belong or fit elsewhere.

In explaining the Zone, even the usually trustworthy *Official Guide Book* had to resort to some tricky dodges and even trickier logic: "Visitors will understand that, in the broad sense, much of the entire Fair is devoted to Community Interests. But here in this Zone are found many of the exhibits which treat more directly with Man's life in a group and his communal interests." (The Gas Exhibit? The Johns-Manville Company Building? The cosmetics exhibit at Maison Coty? Gardens on Parade? The Jewish Palestine Exhibit? The House of Jewels? The Electrified Farm?) No, the Community Interests Zone more or less proved that the whole can sometimes be less than the sum of its parts.

Without a cogent theme to build on, the Focal Exhibit of the Community Interests Zone was in trouble from the beginning. A somewhat windy exposition by Gilbert Rohde, it attempted to show how life had improved since the period of George Washington's inauguration and used everything from animated puppets and projected pictures to mechanical symbols and live actors to do so. Located in the Home Furnishings Building, the Focal Exhibit began with 1789, when human toil claimed sixteen hours a day, and ended with 1939, when labor had been reduced to eight. A coda foretold the near future: Mrs. Modern was shown ordering, by telephone, a house and furnishings complete with a meal to sustain her through the entire day.

"No person of 1939 can live alone; each is a member of the community, whether it be large or small. Every person is caught up in the mesh of its complexities and problems; every person derives immense benefits from his life in the community of his fellow men." No one disagreed with these abstract sentiments, but it still came as no surprise when, in 1940, the Focal Exhibit became "America at Home" and featured model rooms by various interior designers.

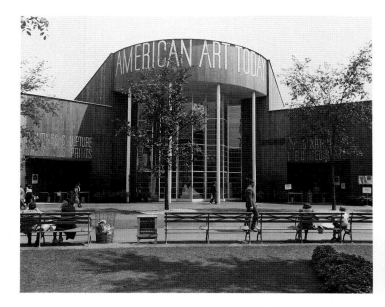

The Contemporary Art Building, which in 1940 was renamed American Art Today, was designed in American redwood by Frederick L. Ackerman, Joshua D. Lowenfish, and John V. Van Pelt. Including works of art selected by a committee headed by the president of the Museum of Modern Art, the exhibit was at the time the most representative exhibition of the work of living American painters, sculptors, and printmakers ever assembled.

The Temple of Religion, shown in rear and front views *above*, was erected by lay representatives of the Catholic, Protestant, and Jewish faiths as a "symbol of the individual's belief in God, irrespective of the form of that belief." Designed by Poor, Stine & Reagan, it included an auditorium that held 1,200 people. On the structure's upper façade were the words, "For All Who Worship God and Prize Religious Freedom."

The Hall of Special Events (*below*) was originally intended to serve as a special exhibition hall for textiles, hence the inclusion of the abstract sheet-steel sculpture at the right side of the façade—*Textiles* by Robert Foster. At the far right twin light towers.

Designed by J. Gordon Carr, with interiors by Donald Deskey, the House of Jewels (*top*) was one of the most popular displays at the Fair. And no wonder. The pavilion gave a Depression public intrigued by the antics of such well-publicized heiresses as Brenda Frazier and Barbara Hutton the chance to see the baubles of the rich up close. With a list of participants that included Tiffany & Co. and Cartier, the display included a 128½-carat yellow diamond, a 109-carat emerald, and a shoulder clip with 700 diamonds.

Surmounted by a huge powder box which announced the building's purpose, the Maison Coty pavilion, designed by Walter Cross, Eliot Cross, and John Hironimus, featured interiors by Donald Deskey that were the equal of the spectacular beauty salon set in MGM's *The Women*. This was the place to go, *The New York Times* urged its distaff readers, if a woman needed to repair her damaged complexion.

The American Radiator and Standard Sanitary Corporation Building (*left*) was constructed with the materials of the industry it represented. Columns were made of flue linings, with Ionic capitals of copper coils from a water heater. At one end of the building was a grille of copper pipe and radiators. The building, by Voorhees, Walker, Foley and Smith, featured the latest in kitchen and bathroom appliances and was known as the American Standard Building in 1940.

Below: Displays for Anthracite Industries, Incorporated, and Keasbey & Mattison Company, an asbestos manufacturer, both located in the Home Building Center.

Not everything in the World of Tomorrow turned out as wonderful as predicted. The Johns-Manville Sales Corporation Building, designed by Shreve, Lamb & Harmon, was dedicated to asbestos, "the magic mineral." In the main foyer of the building, a gigantic figure clad in an asbestos suit was shown in the act of stepping from a flaming pit. It symbolized man's ability to protect himself from heat and fire through the use of "the magic mineral." Fifty years later we are still exorcising ourselves of that white magic.

What had been called Gas Exhibits, Inc. in 1939 became Gas Wonderland in 1940. With virtually every American and Canadian gas utility and appliance manufacturer participating, the exhibit did everything it could to rival the spectacular shows put on by the electrical suppliers and manufacturers in the Production and Distribution Zone. But, given the nature of the product, there was little that could excite audiences without endangering life and limb. The building, however, was something else again. Designed by Skidmore & Owings and John Moss, it was nothing short of wonderful. It included both a main exhibit hall (*above*) and a Court of Flame (*left*), with a perpetual burning flame and surrounded by four 90-foot pylons from which blue and yellow flames soared skyward at night.

Designed by Harrison & Fouilhoux and complete in every detail, the deservedly popular Electrified Farm (*left*) dramatized the advantages of labor-saving machinery for the modern farmer and farm wife. There was nothing Buck Rogersish about the application of electricity to the operation of this carefully planned farm; everything was practical and immediately attainable. This was equally true of the two-story modern farmhouse, where home economists demonstrated the all-electric kitchen by cooking, canning, and preserving.

The Town of Tomorrow consisted of fifteen houses, ranging in style from traditional to streamlined moderne, that were designed to answer the problem of private housing in Depression America. A booklet was given away at each house (*below*), describing the plan and materials used.

CHAPTER TEN

The Government Zone

The Italian Pavilion, designed by Michele Busiri-Vici, was an attention-grabber, all right. Too light to be called "Mussolini modern," too heavy to be called "classical," it was dominated by the Fair's highest waterfall, which ran completely down its stepped façade, and was topped by a figure called "Roma" that looked peculiarly like Britannia. Fairgoers loved it for its almost operatic sense of drama, but architectural critics were largely appalled. "A curious perversion of classical precedent," was *Architectural Forum's* verdict. The well-heeled, however, flocked to the pavilion's luxurious restaurant, modeled on the dining salon of the S.S. Conte di Savoia and one of the most expensive at the Fair.

In June 1936, with pockets of war already ablaze in Europe, Asia, and Africa, Congress authorized President Franklin Delano Roosevelt "to invite the nations of the world to participate in the New York World's Fair." In December, Governor Herbert E. Lehman of New York extended the invitation to the states and territories. In all, fifty-nine foreign governments (and the League of Nations) and thirty-three states were represented, making the New York World's Fair "the most international fair in the long history of expositions." In May 1937, the *Bureau International des Expositions* recognized the Fair as the official international exposition of 1939.

The *Official Guide Book* proclaimed that "the presence of sixty foreign participants makes the Fair a true parliament of the world. Here the peoples of the world unite in amity and understanding, impelled by a friendly rivalry and working toward a common purpose: to set forth their achievements of today and their contribution to the 'World of Tomorrow.' The Fair is a force for peace in the world; for without peace a dream of a better 'World of Tomorrow' is but a cruel and mocking illusion."

The possibility that peace was elusive and that the World of Tomorrow might well be an illusion hung like a cloud over the Fair from the beginning. And that cloud was Nazi Germany, conspicuous at the Fair by its absence. Germany had in fact contracted for a pavilion in 1937, but, faced with increasingly vocal protests from anti-Nazi groups in America, withdrew from its commitment in April 1938, claiming that it could not raise the capital for construction.

In the fall of 1936, the Soviet Union became the first foreign nation to sign a contract for space at the Fair, and was soon joined by Italy, Great Britain, France, Poland, and Japan, all of whom were to be combatants in the war to come. That a Hall of Nations, central to the plan of the Government Zone, should have been erected about a Court of Peace is one of the unwitting ironies of the New York World's Fair.

Still, the Government Zone, with its monumental buildings, handsomely proportioned courts, and acres of colorfully unfurling flags, was one of the most visually exciting areas of the Fair. No one could have predicted Germany's invasion of Poland on September 1, 1939, nor could anyone have predicted what that and subsequent events would do to change the very nature of the Fair in 1940. After the Russian Pavilion was dismantled in the winter of 1939, it was replaced—as nation after nation fell to the Germans in 1940—by a place of pageantry called the American Commons. Almost overnight, "the most international fair" had been turned into an American county fair by Adolf Hitler.

The arrangement of exhibition buildings that made up the Court of States (*above*) was anchored at one end of the reflecting pool by the Virginia Building. The same function was served at the opposite end by the Pennsylvania Building (*opposite page*), a replica of Philadelphia's Independence Hall. The entrance to the Court of States (*right*) was decorated with Ezra Winter's mural, "United States Industries," in which figures bearing appropriate symbols depicted America's chief industries. Although the exterior of the Pennsylvania Building was dramatically Colonial, the interior was handsomely modern. The "Bridge of Unity" (*opposite page*), a curved steel structure suspended from the ceiling, provided a view of the exhibits in the Hall of Democracy and the Hall of Tradition.

CONRAD H. RUPPERT

THE COURT OF STATES

With two exceptions, the exhibits of the American states were grouped in and around the Court of States near the United States Building and the Lagoon of Nations. The exceptions were Florida, which had a special building in the Amusement Area, and New York, which owned the amphitheater on the shores of Fountain Lake housing the Aquacade and the exhibition building just behind it. The Court of States was a special group of buildings arranged around a long reflecting pool, the architecture emphasizing three traditional types—the Georgian, the French, and the Spanish—to symbolize the three major settlers of Colonial America. Because of this national theme, the Court of States was the only area of the Fair where the Board of Design relaxed its requirement of original architecture and permitted traditional design.

Participating states included Arizona, Arkansas, Florida, Georgia, Illinois, Maine, New England (a group exhibit for Connecticut, Massachusetts, New Hampshire, Rhode Island, and Vermont), Missouri, Nevada, New Jersey, New York, North Carolina, Ohio, Pennsylvania, Tennessee, Texas, Utah, Virginia, Washington, and West Virginia. Additional exhibits included those of Puerto Rico and New York City.

Opposite page: The Government Zone of the Fair was dominated by the United States Building (also called the Federal Building), which stood at the head of the Court of Peace. Designed by Howard L. Cheyney, the monumental structure was rich in symbolism: the two massive towers signified the judiciary and legislative branches of government; the central section stood for the executive; thirteen columns between the towers represented the thirteen original states. The towers were embellished by Harry Poole Camden's sculptures, "Peace" and "Unity."

In tribute to George Washington, whose inauguration in 1787 was the ostensible reason for the Fair, the New Jersey Building was a replica of the "Old Barracks," where Hessian troops were defeated in the Battle of Trenton by Washington's forces.

This page: Made of native woods, with towering bronze pillars, the Washington Building featured displays of the state's industry, sports, and scenic beauty and a scale model of the Grand Coulee Dam. Washington was the only West Coast state to exhibit at the Fair.

MELVILLE DAVID WEINGARTEN

The New York City Building, now the home of the Queens Museum, was designed as a permanent structure by Aymar Embury II. Among its features were "Murder at Midnight," a drama showcasing the skills of the city's police department, and demonstrations of the collective prowess of the fire department.

CONRAD H. RUPPERT

Five New England states cooperated in the New England Combined Exhibit, which consisted of a reproduction of a wharf and dockside warehouse and a replica of a seagoing schooner which brought the trade goods of the world to such a wharf in the great days of New England sail. Within this setting, each state—Connecticut, Massachusetts, New Hampshire, Rhode Island, and Vermont—maintained a separate hall for displays of state history, industry, and tourism.

The Classical Revival façade of the Missouri Building was a replica of one of the state's historic landmarks—the Rolls County Courthouse, erected at New London, Missouri, in 1856. As in other state pavilions, displays varied widely from history to agriculture, industry, and education. Of particular interest was Missouri's tribute to her native sons, Mark Twain, Thomas Hart Benton, and Carl Schurz.

With its miles of sunny beaches and stately Spanish Colonial resorts (peppered in the 1930s by aggressively urban Art Deco hotels), Florida sensed a vast market for tourism at the New York World's Fair. With its intention of re-creating no less than a strip of tropical beach in Flushing Meadows, Florida was separated from its sister states on the Court of States and built its pavilion, the largest of the state exhibits, on the west side of Fountain Lake. The description of the exhibit in the *Official Guide Book* is picture-perfect in its period flavor:

"On the lake shore is a typical Florida beach, gay with palmetto shelters, colored umbrellas, tons of Florida sand, a smart cabana club, and bathing beauties in beach togs. Palms and orange trees loaded with fruit, and 6,000 tropical plantings including an orchid jungle from the Everglades, make a luxurious background for the beach, the exhibit building, surmounted by a carillon tower, and for the garden and patio . . . On the lake, experts in bait-casting show you how easy it is to snare a giant fish . . . In the evening, wrought-iron lamps throw a soft light over the beach, music plays, fun goes on in the cabana club, and you watch the brilliant fireworks show on the lake from the 1,000 foot boardwalk . . . Orange juice, grapefruit juice, and sherbets are served in the building, on the beach and in the beach club, which, incidentally, has two play decks for the energetic."

The beach club was fronted by a talking statue of Ponce de Leon that startled fairgoers by inviting them to come in.

THE HALL OF NATIONS—

Lining two sides of the Court of Peace, one end of the Lagoon of Nations, and one side each of Presidential Rows North and South were seven groups of attached buildings given the collective name of the Hall of Nations. Each building was divided into separate exhibition halls, with individual entrances crowned by symbolic statues representing participating nations. Particularly as these uniform buildings appeared along the Court of Peace, each displaying colorful national flags, and with the United States Building dominating one end of the Court (*opposite page*), the impression given was one of world unity with the United States in full command.

Prophetically, the League of Nations, then in its final days as a world organization, built its pavilion (*right*) at a location in the Government Zone far removed from the Hall of Nations. It was simultaneously the first and last time the League exhibited at an international fair.

Opposite page: The majestic curves of the French Pavilion formed an immense glass bay with a wide terrace overlooking the Lagoon of Nations. Designed by the firm of Expert & Patout, the pavilion featured a spectacular sweeping staircase in an immense hall decorated with Gobelin tapestries; a mezzanine art gallery of paintings, sculptures, ceramics, lacquer, carpets, china, and other French arts and crafts; a museum of peasant life, illustrating the cultures of Alsace, Brittany, and Provençe; an auditorium showing French films; and a restaurant that was probably the finest at the Fair.

In the Hall of Nations was a second French exhibit, devoted to French colonies, protectorates, and mandates and the characteristic products and crafts of each. Within the hall of the French Overseas Building was the "Planisphere," a lighted map of the world indicating France's overseas possessions.

This page: With its stone balconies, high beamed ceiling, and long windows, Romanian House—designed by Prince George Cantacuzino and Octav Doicescu—was modeled after rural monasteries and was built of marble from Ruschitza, with alabaster balustrades lighted internally. Within the pavilion were displays of Romanian textiles, ceramics, rugs, furniture, painting, and sculpture, used primarily as a setting for a Romanian restaurant serving food prepared by chefs from Bucharest to the accompaniment of Gypsy violins.

Much admired by architectural critics was the Argentine Pavilion, designed by Armando D'Ans who also created his nation's pavilion at the Golden Gate Exposition in San Francisco. Particularly appreciated was the striking manner in which the flavor of Argentina's modern architecture had been retained in a temporary building, the strong overhangs, the use of tempered plate glass doors (still a novelty in 1939), and the circular skylights in the ceiling of the main exhibit hall. The inner walls of the entrance hall were composed of glass showcases, giving visitors both inside and out a clear view of many displays, and a large mural by Alfredo Guido, representing Argentina's social and historical aspects, was visible from the handsomely landscaped gardens.

Anyone who went to the Netherlands exhibit expecting to find quaint windmills, Dutch maidens, and wooden shoes was not reckoning on the Netherlands' tradition of pioneering modern architecture. Designed by Dirk F. Slothouwer and George B. Post & Sons, the Netherlands Pavilion was distinguished by its impressive entrance court, which sheltered a statue of Peter Stuyvesant, colonial governor of New Amsterdam, beneath tall and narrow columns. At night these columns—glass-faced and filled with fluorescent tubing—turned the entire structure into a luminous unit. The exhibits inside were devoted to city planning, social welfare, science, agriculture, and government, all set forth by murals, photographs, models, and charts. The Dutch overseas possessions were made graphic in murals and dioramas, including an animated model sixty feet long which showed the daily work of coffee, tea, rice, and tapioca farmers in Java. Of particular interest was a large relief map, complete with canals, dikes, and, yes, windmills, which was alternately flooded and drained in a miniature drama of Dutch land reclamation.

Designed by Van de Velde, Stynen, and Bourgois, the Belgian Pavilion was made entirely of Belgian materials (red tile with black slate) and was marked by a 155-foot carillon tower in which were thirty-six bronze bells cast in Tournai by Jef Dedyn, master *carilloneur*. In the monumental reception hall were modern tapestries designed by Floris Jespers with scenes from Belgian history. Exhibits, which *Architectural Forum* called "drab and inferior," included Belgian linens, laces, precision instruments, and cutlery. A Belgian Congo display was devoted to tropical woods, palm oil, radium, and diamonds.

Surprisingly, Henry Luce's *Architectural Forum* had nothing but praise for Boris M. Iofan's and Karo S. Alabian's Union of Soviet Socialist Republics Building: "Rated first among the foreign pavilions in a recent Gallup poll, the building of the Soviet Union is a powerful, if occasionally naive, piece of monumental architecture. Designed for rebuilding as a museum in Moscow, it makes lavish use of such permanent materials as marble and granite. The symmetrical plan works well for moving crowds, and there is an open-air cinema to take the overflow. Best exhibit: a full-size section of a Moscow subway station, given the effect of a complete interior by the use of mirrors." Shown at the top of this page is the mammoth lobby painting by eleven Soviet painters, a 42 by 30-foot group portrait of fifty prominent Russian figures.

The Portuguese Building, designed by Antonio Lopez and Jorge Segurado, was a curious blend of ancient and modern that was almost startling in its discordance. A stylized medieval castle with 1930s ribbon-strip windows was appended to a glass-enclosed rectangle, housing a colorful mosaic mural. The displays inside were far more conventional than the building that sheltered them and were devoted largely to early Portuguese exploration and colonization, and to tourism.

"One of the most interesting architectural contributions in Flushing Meadows," wrote *Architectural Forum*, "is the tower of the Polish Pavilion, a lacy metal structure covered with gilded plaques." Designed by Jan Cybulski and Jan Galinowski, the building devoted much of its interior space to exhibits emphasizing Poland's democratic constitution, almost as old as the United States Constitution. Other displays dealt with Polish science, culture, and industry, as well as the role Poles played in the building of America.

CONRAD H. RUPPERT

CONRAD H. RUPPERT

After Germany invaded Poland on September 1, 1939, the Polish Pavilion became a mecca for fairgoers concerned with the possibility that the world of tomorrow promised the end of modern civilization. Instead of the usually gay pamphlets distributed as exhibition souvenirs, visitors to the pavilion received the set of photographic reproductions showing the destruction of Poland illustrated here. Even the *Official Guide Book* for 1940, which did everything possible to ignore the war, dealt with the tragedy of Poland, albeit symbolically: "Every evening at dusk, a horn call sounds out loud and clear above the tumult of the Fair—then stops suddenly on a broken note. This is the "Hejnal," blown from the top of Poland's golden Pavilion tower, commemorating the death of a Polish watchman who, centuries ago, saved the city of Krakow from invaders. He fell dead with an arrow in his throat, the unfinished warning ending on a broken, jarred note . . . a broken note symbolical of the story of Poland."

This page: "Remembering the smorgasbord," wrote *The New York Times,* "it is easy to understand why the Swedish Pavilion is in the Food Zone rather than in the Government Zone. But the Three Crowns Restaurant, managed by the Swedish American Line, is only a part of the exhibit that portrays Swedish life and social progress." The refreshingly simple and unpretentious pavilion was designed by Sven Markelius and Pomerance & Breines and was arranged around a large courtyard paved in marble. Within the reflecting pool of the courtyard was a ten-foot fountain of Orrefors crystal, designed by Vicke Lindstrand. Surrounding the courtyard were one-story loggias which housed many of the exhibits.

In 1939 the Canadian Pavilion was overlooked by almost everyone writing about the Fair. Its very ordinariness rendered it instantly forgettable. Today the F. W. Williams-designed pavilion emerges from anonymity as a rare example of Fair architecture that actually looked like everyday buildings of the period. There's very little fantasy here, just straightforward curves and horizontal windows breaking the verticality of the portico, as was common in the late 1930s. The interiors, however, were a dreary replay of the Canadian image foisted upon the world by Hollywood's *Rose Marie,* and there might have been one too many Nelson Eddy look-alike Mounties for comfort.

Opposite page; Many readers were aghast when *Architectural Forum* declared that the British Pavilion was "an attempt to combine British good taste with totalitarian monumentality." But half a century later that distinguished magazine's judgment still seems critically sound. Not that the fairgoers of 1939 cared. They loved the building and patiently queued to see the replicas of the Crown jewels, the copy of the Magna Carta, and the family tree of George Washington, showing the first president's direct descent from King John. Many other exhibits were on display in the massive halls of the pavilion, designed by Stanley Hall and Easton & Robertson. The photograph of the pavilion's main entrance was taken on the occasion of the visit of King George VI and Queen Elizabeth, June 10, 1939.

This page: Located in the Community Interests Zone, and designed by Arieh El-Hanani and Norvin R. Lindheim, the Jewish Palestine Pavilion was sponsored by sixty-one organizations interested in the establishment of a Jewish homeland in the Holy Land. The pavilion's exhibits showed how Jewish settlers had reclaimed swamps and irrigated deserts and emphasized creative achievements in culture, social programs, and colonization. (In this illustration a bust of Theodore Herzl is unveiled before the pavilion's main entrance.) Times change. The 1939 *Official Guide Book* justified the existence of the pavilion by calling it "an answer to the charge of unproductiveness levelled against the Jew."

Those who expected the usual Irish sentiment and crafts from the Eire Pavilion weren't disappointed, but the building itself was something of a shock. What housed Irish linens, woolens, pottery, and lace was one of the most successful examples of modern architecture at the Fair. Michael Scott's building was shaped like a shamrock, with the stem curving as entrance. And it boasted a spectacular spiral staircase in addition to vast expanses of glass.

Opposite page: In a pavilion modeled after an ancient Shinto shrine, and designed by Y. Utida and Yasuo Matsui, Japan stressed her history, her culture, and her friendly relations with the United States, rather than her industries. The most unusual item on display was a $1 million model of the Liberty Bell, made of silver and encrusted with pearls and diamonds. Shown here is a detail of the pavilion and its magnificent grand hall.

Opposite page: Like several other countries that exhibited at the Fair, Turkey maintained two separate locations and displays—an individual pavilion of her own, and an additional building within the Hall of Nations. THe Turkish Exhibit in the Hall of Nations was a largely symbolic expression of the rise of modern Turkey under Kemal Atatürk, who had only recently died. Within the large, starkly modern hall (*left*) was a cascade on one side of which was represented Asia, with Europe on the other. A statue of a man holding a knotted rope symbolized the new Turkey, linking the two continents and helping to preserve world peace. The Turkish Pavilion, an essentially modern structure made to appear traditional by its use of exotic tilework and overhanging eaves, was located in the Food Zone—and not without reason. Native foods were prominently on display, and the pavilion—designed by Sidad H. Eldem and Sedat Zinciskiran—housed one of the better restaurants at the Fair.

Right: Fifty years after the New York World's Fair, the interior of Alvar Aalto's Finnish Pavilion is still considered one of the few acknowledged architectural masterpieces of the Fair. "The Fair's most exciting demonstration of what can be done with a bare rectantgular room," *Architectural Forum* called it, and other critics agreed. Meant to suggest "a flaming Aurora Borealis," an inner wall of three wood curtains used photographic enlargements incorporated into the design to project the resources, people, and labor of Finland. Sadly, the exhibit was meant to promote the 1940 Olympics in Helsinki, an event that was not to be.

The pavilion that William Lescaze and John R. Weber designed for Switzerland combined modern and traditional elements. Built around the pleasant open-air restaurant which was its chief attraction, it contained exhibits devoted to Swiss watches and winter sports, as well as the inevitable demonstrations of cheese making. The trouble was that the Swiss kitsch was laid on with a trowel, both in the pavilion proper and in the subsidiary exhibit in the Hall of Nations. Aside from the yodeling, much of the exhibit was coy rather than clever: "In the textile section, mechanical glamor girls model gowns of Swiss organdies and striking prints. These delicate lovelies are prototypes of the posed figures atop old-fashioned Swiss music boxes. They are full size and utterly adorable. Some of them dance, others walk about, another moves her foot daintily up and down as she relaxes demurely in a chair. One brunette even plays the piano." After that, it was definitely time for the restaurant, even if the meals were served "to the accompaniment of yodeling, alphorn, and hackbrett."

CHAPTER ELEVEN

The Amusement Area

In a word, the nightly fireworks over Fountain Lake (Liberty Lake in 1940) were spectacular. Water fireworks, great set pieces stretching down the lake for a thousand feet, animated pictorial themes, patriotic displays, fountains of fire shooting aloft, star-clusters and flags—nothing was left out.

"'A' is for Amusement," the *Official Guide Book* says, "and in the alphabetical listing of the seven zones of the Fair, it stands first." Strictly speaking, however, the 280-acre site reserved for fun that ran halfway around Fountain Lake was not an official zone at all, but an "area" since it had no focal exhibit. And, while fun may have ranked first in the minds of many who attended the Fair, it often ranked last in the minds of many of its high-minded creators. The result was an Amusement Area that, though relatively free of the force-fed educational content of other zones, was effectively sanitized for the American family. Deprived of a midway, the standard setting of an amusement park, the Amusement Area was permitted the carnival atmosphere of a Coney Island, but not its generic tawdriness. There were to be no Sally Rands, with or without fans. New York preferred its feminine pulchritude *semi*-clothed.

But tastes change, and of what was considered good, clean fun in 1939, much strikes us as vulgar or tasteless or just plain tacky today: "Nature's Mistakes," for example ("animal freaks from the two-headed cow to the pig without a ham. All exhibits are alive. 25¢"); or "Arctic Girls' Temple of Ice" ("comely girls going in for frostbite by wrapping themselves up in ice overcoats. 15¢"); or "Infant Incubator" ("live babies in a scientific nursery with all the latest appliances. 25¢"); or "Amazon Warriors" ("girl athletes in helmets and shields stage a gladiatorial combat, wrestle, throw the javelin. Positively not the Bloomer Girls baseball team. 25¢"); or "N.T.G.'s Congress of Beauty" ("a hundred girls in a Garden of Eden, playing games, riding ponies, taking sun baths. Clad mostly in chiffon leaves. 25¢"). Then there was "Admiral Byrd's Penquin Island," where, for a dime, one could ogle the "little-old-men birds"; "Bel Geddes Mirror Show," where, for fifteen cents, "a single girl appears to be a whole chorus of World's Fairettes"; and penny arcades, and skee ball, and even a replica of Africa's Victoria Falls.

But there was more, much more. (And still more in 1940 when the area was enlarged and renamed "The Great White Way.) There were rides, aqua-shows, Indian villages, music festivals and concerts, dancing, children's playgrounds, fireworks. As the *Official Guide Book* put it, with only minor hyperbole, "By day a mosaic of color, by night a veritable fairyland of light with ample facilities for handling more than 350,000 visitors at one time, the Amusement Area of the New York World's Fair, with its 100 different attractions, has the best claim to being the greatest playground the world has ever seen."

Left: Sun Valley, one of the largest village concessions in the Amusement Area, meant real skiing, real skating, on real snow, real ice. A "winter wonderland," it offered professional performers, mountain scenery, a 40-foot waterfall, toboggans, wandering minstrels, an enormous pipe organ, orchestra, dance platform, more than thirty shops, and several restaurants and bars—and all for a quarter. As *The New York Times* asked, "What more do you want in the Summertime?"

Below: Frank Buck's Jungleland was a press agent's delight. "Frank (Bring 'Em Back Alive) Buck has made his greatest capture. He has brought the whole jungle back alive to the Fair. Here are thousands of rare specimens of wild life from the jungles penetrated by this animal expert." The thatched roofs, rattan flooring, and tree-branch framework were supposed to make the native camp authentic, but just how authentic can be seen from Jungleland's special features: Jiggs, a trained five-year old orangutan; Minnie, the elephant jitterbug; and the three elephant sisters, Trixie, Cutie, and Maud.

Opposite page: Surmounting the National Cash Register Company's exhibit was "the world's largest cash register," a 40-foot model of NCR's deluxe model for 1939. Designed by Walter Dorwin Teague, the giant machine rang up both the daily attendance figures at the Fair and the total attendance to date. Continually revolving so that it could be seen from any part of the surrounding area, the cash register displayed its 2½-foot figures 74 feet in the air. Displays in the building itself included an NCR cash register and all of its 7,857 parts, exhibited under glass.

This page: One of the many clowns that delighted young visitors to Children's World wears a policeman's uniform of the Gay Nineties that is decorated with scores of souvenir pins. Morris Gest's Miracle Town was a complete miniature village, supposedly brought over from Europe, and inhabited by 125 midgets. "Never before," trumpeted the press releases, "has there been a midget village as spectacular as this one." The show cost a quarter, and for an additional sum a visitor could pose with a resident little person for a souvenir photo.

Opposite page: Heineken's on the Zuider Zee was an attractive bit of Holland, complete with windmill and fishing boat, but it was essentially a restaurant where one could dine, drink Heineken beer, and listen to orchestral music.

Old New York (*opposite*) was a nostalgic re-creation of the Gay Nineties that included every cliché from organ grinders and bare-knuckles fights to a 100-foot replica of the Brooklyn Bridge, built so that someone calling himself Steve Brodie could jump off it. Although Dr. William Beebe's famous bathysphere was on display at the New York Zoological Society's building (*below*), the crowds really came to see the cuddly panda and watch an eel illuminate a bulb. For a quarter fairgoers boarded a rocket ship at the Museum of Natural History's Theatre of Time and Space and learned about the stars and planets.

Water ballet did not originate with Billy Rose, Eleanor Holm, or the New York World's Fair. A group of swimming women who called themselves the Modern Mermaids had entertained at the 1933 Century of Progress Exposition and were noted for their ability to eat bananas underwater. But Rose raised the swimming extravaganza to new heights with his famous Aquacade, a sensation at the 1937 Great Lakes Exposition, the 1939-40 New York World's Fair, and the 1940 Golden Gate Exposition. Roses's dripping, half-clad "Aquabeaux" and "Aquabelles" reputedly earned him a very dry $5 million. In the grand finale (*above*) everything but the grand piano twirled, kicked, splashed, bowed, or threw off patriotic bunting. Audiences loved it. At the *right* is the cover of the souvenir program.

"American Jubilee" was a new entertainment for 1940, and the hyperventilated prose of the *Official Guide Book* describes the show quite accurately: "America strides the stage in this romantic, song-spun spectacle fusing history, musical comedy, circus, opera, and pageant. The great names of the entertainment world are here—Arthur Schwartz, Oscar Hammerstein II, Leon Leonidoff of Radio City Music Hall, and Albert Johnson. They've blended their talents in a star-spangled spectacle rivalling anything the theatre has seen in scope and splendor. Three hundred performers and forty trained horses take part . . . and you can see it for forty cents."

Above, clockwise from lower left: Among the Broadway shows brought to the Fair were *The Hot Mikado,* the all-black swing version of Gilbert and Sullivan's comic opera, and *Streets of Paris,* starring Gypsy Rose Lee and Abbott and Costello. Merrie Old England, of which the Old Curiosity Shop was but a corner, did for Britain in 1939 what Busch Gardens does for the rest of the world today: you can travel abroad without ever leaving home. The Ballantine Three-Ring Inn was an informal restaurant that seated 2,000 diners and offered twenty main courses, but only one brand of beer. The Lama Temple was a reproduction of an ancient Jehol shrine.

Opposite page: Based on a device used to train military parachutists, the Parachute Jump was the most popular ride at the Fair. The 250-foot descent cost a stiff forty cents.

CHAPTER TWELVE

Sculpture

The façade of Salvador Dali's surrealistic fantasy, "Dream of Venus" (or "Living Pictures"), was covered with evocative sculptures. In fact much of the exhibit included works that could be called sculptural, the couch in the shape of Mae West's lips being the most notorious. Although the Museum of Modern Art had hosted the famous surrealism show three years earlier, the average New Yorker was still not ready for Dali in 1939. Dali's "Dream of Venus" did not reappear in 1940. Shown here is the artist's sketch of the exhibit's phantasmagoric façade.

Since architecture is universally acknowledged to be "the parent of the arts," any understanding of the widespread presence of sculpture at the New York World's Fair must begin with the rules governing the design of the Fair's buildings themselves. As Frank Monaghan wrote in *The Official Souvenir Book* of 1939, "the architectural scheme of the Fair was executed with the aim of frankly expressing the temporary nature of the buildings and at the same time maintaining complete aesthetic harmony in the architectural, sculptural, and landscaping plan. By way of contrast with the skyscrapers of adjacent New York, Fair buildings consist largely of windowless, one-story structures, artificially illuminated and ventilated. The barren aspect of blank surfaces was overcome through the application of sculpture, murals, and shadows cast by appropriately arranged vines and trees. The result is 'unity without uniformity.'"

Since the Fair buildings varied so in their conformity with the Board of Design's ground rules, infinite variety in artistic conception and technique was embodied in the scores of sculptured pieces by which the leading sculptors of the 1930s were represented at the Fair. More than sixty commissioned pieces, heroic in size, adorned the various buildings, thoroughfares, and plazas, with many more included in the decor of the commercial and governmental exhibits. Dominated by James Earle Fraser's huge statue of George Washington, the greatest concentration of sculpture was centered on Constitution Mall.

"Everywhere," wrote Monaghan, "the sculptured works fit into the Fair's general theme, giving expression to the particular section of the exposition in which they are located. In the Transportation Zone, for instance, (are) 'The Spirit of the Wheel' by René P. Chambellan and 'Riders of the Elements' by Chester Beach, symbols of man's progress in transportation. In the Court of Communications, Joseph Reniers's 'Speed'—a woman astride a winged horse—suggests the rapidity with which man's thoughts may be carried around the world by modern means of communication, while on the facade of the Administration Building 'Mithrana' by Albert Stewart portrays the Spirit of the Fair unveiling the future."

Most of the sculptures at the Fair were made of plaster, but outstanding exceptions included Robert Foster's "Textiles," a thirty-foot female figure fashioned from sheets of steel; Lawrence Tenny Stevens's "Tree of Life," carved from an elm trunk forty-five feet high; and Waylande Gregory's "Fountain of the Atom," made of ceramic tiles surrounded by a shaft of glass brick.

In all, thirty-five sculptors were commissioned by the Fair Corporation. A selection of their work appears in the pages that follow.

Opposite page: The enormous theme statue of George Washington in his in-augural robes by James Earle Fraser, and John Quincy Ward's "Seal of Protection" for the Equitable Life Assurance Company pavilion.

This page: "Time," Joseph Kiselewski's trellis sundial between the two sections of the Business Systems and Insurance Building, and "Textiles," Robert Foster's sheet-steel figure outside the Hall of Special Events.

Overleaf, page 180: Three of the four sculptures by Paul Manship for his "Moods of Time" fountain on Constitution Mall—"Day," "Morning," and "Night."

Overleaf, page 181: John Gregory's "Victories of Peace"—representing Wheels, Wings, Wheat, and Wisdom —a sculpture group in the Court of Power.

This page: Gertrude Vanderbilt Whitney's "To the Morrow" was called "Wings" by most people, possibly because of the 24-foot wingspan of the sculpture, possibly because Fiorello LaGuardia called it a tribute to aviation at its dedication. Whitney herself said that its theme was Youth.

With most pavilions windowless to increase exhibition space, sculptures were frequently applied to buildings to relieve open space. Pictured here is one of the many sculptures placed over the entrances to the Railroads Building.

Opposite page: Within the rotunda of the League of Nations Building, four murals powerfully depicted War, Famine, Pestilence, and Exile as conditions of the modern world. These were offset by five sculptures representing Justice, Order, Freedom, Security, and Peace.

"The Open Road," Jo Davidson's sculptured figure of Walt Whitman, took its title from the poet's line, "Strong and content I travel the open road."

Representing "benevolence," Edmond Amateis's sculpture of the famous midwestern itinerant preacher "Johnny Appleseed," was one of three sections of an American folklore group adorning the façade of the Medicine and Public Health Building. The evangelist Jonathan Chapman, a real character who became a legend, is shown in typical action, handing out apple seeds accompanied by a sermon as he wandered barefoot across America dressed in a coffee sack and wearing a kitchen utensil for a hat.

"Europa" by Gleb Derujinsky occupied the center of a pool at the intersection of the Court of Railways and Transportation Avenue in front of the Railroad Building.

"American Manhood" (*below*) was one of a pair of statues created by Gaetano Cecere for the Bowling Green façade of the Home Furnishings Building. The companion piece represented American womanhood.

"Dances of the Races," a huge relief in the form of a drum by Malvina Hoffmann, stood in the center of the Spiral Garden between the Hall of Pharmacy and the New York City Building.

"Riders of the Elements" by Chester Beach was placed at the intersection of the Court of Ships and the Avenue of Transportation.

This page: "Samson and the Lion," a sculptural group by Benjamin Hawkins, stood just before Corona Gate South. (The Ford Building is in the background.)

Dominating the Court of Communications, which extended from the Trylon and Perisphere to the Communications Building, was a figure of a woman astride a winged horse. Joseph Renier's "Speed" was meant to suggest the speed of modern communications. The basic motif of the sculptural group is the horizontal line, which is both expressive of the theme and indicative of decorative sculpture of the 1930s.

Opposite page: Leo Friedlander's four statues representing the "Four Freedoms"—freedom of Speech, Religion, Press, and Assembly—stood on Constitution Mall behind the statue of George Washington, near the Lagoon of Nations. (Shown in close-up is the 30-foot "Freedom of Speech.")

This page: "Builders of the Future" (*above, left*), a sculpture by William Zorach in the Court of Roses, was intended to suggest "tomorrow's builders, their aspirations and ideals."

"Manhattan," a sculpture group by Sidney Waugh (*above, right*), stood at the center of a fountain before the main entrance to the Marine Transportation Building.

The sculptured female figure reaching upward with a ball represented "The Spirit of Florida." Set in the center of a circular arcade and surrounded by cactus plants and orange trees, the statue was set in the patio of the Florida Building.

Opposite page: Near the Trylon and Perisphere, on Constitution Mall, stood the sculptural sundial called "Time and the Fates of Man" by Paul Manship. The sculpture represented "the Tree of Life, the Three Fates, and Man's Destiny."

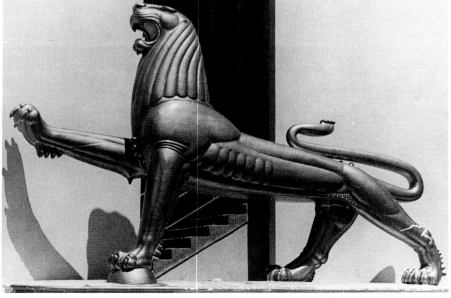

Opposite page: Before the curved gateway leading to the main courtyard of the American Telephone & Telegraph Building was the sculptural group "The Pony Express" by Carl Milles, representing communication of the past.

Admired by almost every person who visited the Fair, and remembered with fondness by many to this day, are the stylized lions that guarded the main entrance of the British Pavilion. The lions were designed by A. F. Hardiman.

This page: Located in a garden flanking the right wing of the Contemporary Arts Building was Augusta Savage's "The Harp" (also known as "Lift Every Voice and Sing"). The frame of the harp represented the hand of God; the strings, blacks singing.

Paul Manship's "Celestial Sphere" rotated on the backs of four turtles above a reflecting pool in the Court of States. It was a replica of a bronze sculpture executed by Manship in front of the League of Nations Building in Geneva and commissioned by the Woodrow Wilson Foundation.

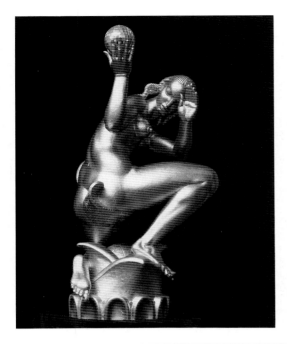

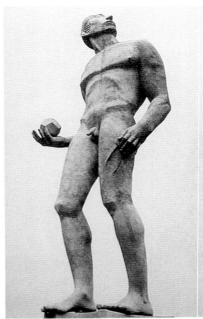

Raymond Barger's "Goddess of Perfection" crowned the tallest sculptural group at the Fair and was located within the Heinz Dome in 1939 and atop the Dome itself in 1940.

Located near the Perisphere was "The Astronomer" (sometimes called "The Star-Gazer") by Carl Milles, a Swedish-born sculptor whose works were well received in the United States after his arrival in 1929.

"Golden Sprays" by Leo Lentelli represented American beauty, the "product of a healthy environment which gives due importance to recreation and exercise." Appropriately, the 11-foot-high sculpture stood in the Court of Sports.

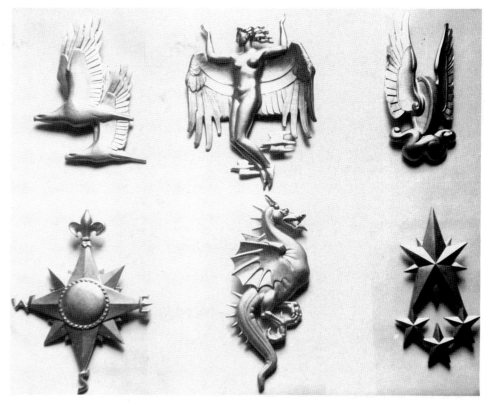

Separating the Court of Power from the Plaza of Light were four 65-foot pylons representing the four elements. Adorning these pylons were forty-eight relief sculptures by Carl Paul Jennewein, six of which are illustrated to the *left*.

Chassis Fountain dominated one section of the Ford Building's garden court. Located inside the spiral ramp of "The Road of Tomorrow," the fountain was surrounded by flower beds and trees. The fountain, "designed to express the feeling of power in the Ford V-8 engine," was the work of Isamu Noguchi.

"Tree of Life," one of the largest wooden statues in the world, was carved for the Fair by Lawrence Tenney Stevens from an elm planted by Hessian prisoners of the Revolutionary War in South Windsor, Connecticut. It was 63 feet high and represented "a great ethereal spirit, dominating the center of a three-figured group. The sculptor carved two companion pieces from red eucalyptus wood, depicting "Man" and "Woman" in search of truth.

in 1939
THE
NEW YORK WORLD'S FAIR
CULIN
COPYRIGHT 1937, NEW YORK WORLD'S FAIR 1939 INCORPORATED

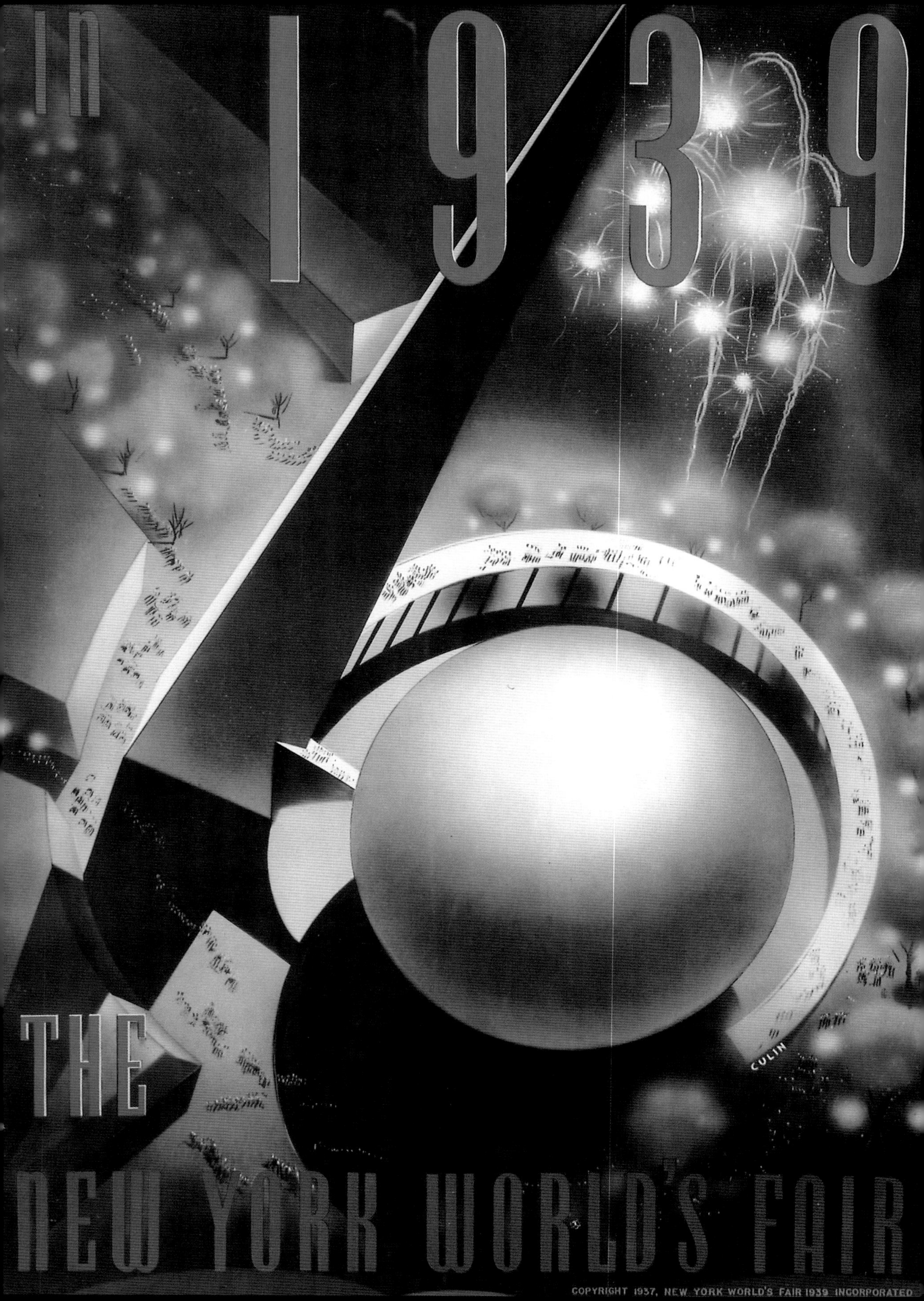

CHAPTER THIRTEEN

The Merchandise of Tomorrow: World's Fair Memorabilia

In October 1936, Robert Kohn, chairman of the New York World's Fair committee on theme, announced that the 1939 Fair would be "a consumer's fair . . . oriented toward the non-technical person . . . in terms that could be understood by the average person, so that he could find something which would mean something in his own life. Something which he could have if he goes after it." What the average visitor "could have if he (went) after it" was not only the material offerings of General Motors, RCA, and Westinghouse, displayed so brilliantly in futuristic pavilions, but also the thousands of material goods designed especially for the Fair and sold there and in selected stores. These goods were described in the *Official Guide Book* as the products of "farsighted designers and manufacturers who have seized the opportunity afforded by the New York World's Fair. They have produced new products and molded new plans to meet a *new* demand, because they know that the Fair will affect, if not completely change, the desires and tastes of the sixty million that will visit the Fair this year." But Grover Whalen, who had an even better way with words, called the ashtrays and vases, the dishes and glassware, "the merchandise of tomorrow."

Thus, the New York World's Fair was filled with things to buy, useful and useless souvenirs for the fairgoer to spend his money on. Fifty years later, this "merchandise of tomorrow" is still being bought, when it can be found, but in a market growing tighter and more expensive by the day.

Although, such substantial objects as radios, electric shavers, typewriters, and electric fans were sold to commemorate the Fair, as the pages that follow will attest, most of the hundreds of designs devised for the event, and produced under license as souvenirs, were made of the most common materials—plastics, china, cheap metals, and paper. Despite this—perhaps because of it—collectors never tire of seeking every object they can find that was a product of the extravaganza at Flushing Meadows.

As the more substantial objects begin to disappear from view, the more common souvenirs will appeal to collectors even more. In fact the Trylon and Perisphere salt and pepper shakers, the key cases, compacts, drinking glasses, paper napkins, candles, spoons, cameras, license plates, coasters, mirrors, teapots, pitchers, tie clips, bracelets, pens, and postcards are far more likely than the disappearing rarities to trigger shock waves of nostalgia in all old enough to remember the Fair and its vision of tomorrow. And for those too young to have known the Fair, just to see these objects, if not to own them, is to have a more intimate relationship with the past.

Many kitchens of the 1930s had a combination dining table-work table with matching chairs. This kitchen set by an unidentified maker used the Trylon and Perisphere as an incised motif on the decorative stretcher of the table, on the chair backs, and (in orange and blue) on the folding metal work top. Closed, the unpainted oak table measures 25″ deep and 40″ long. Similar sets were available painted white, with orange and blue Perispheres and Trylons.

The Adam Hat Company decorated its hatboxes with a white Trylon and Perisphere against a blue background with orange trim. The boxes came in various sizes.

Both the clip that held the cord and the Remington Close-Shaver itself were decorated with a rendering of the Electrical Products Building, which housed the Remington Rand exhibit in 1939. The Close-Shaver ran on either AC or DC power and featured a molded plastic cord, an unusual advance for the time.

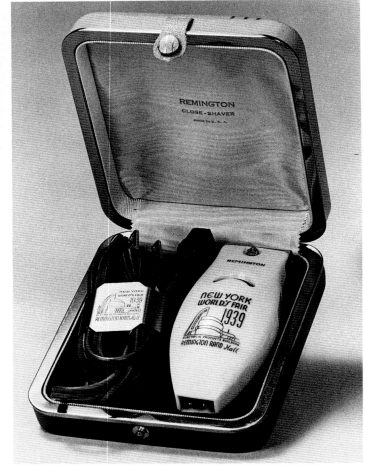

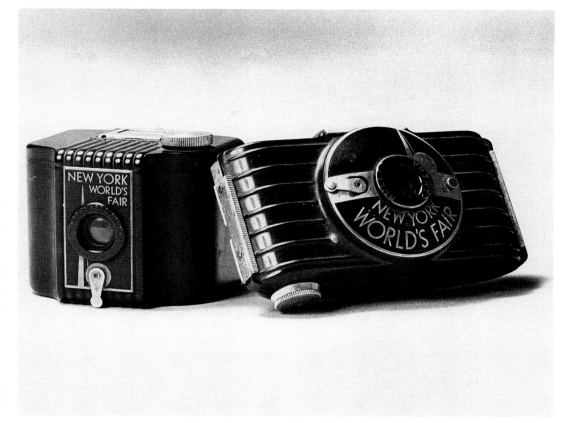

The addition of the words "NEW YORK WORLD'S FAIR" and an applied Trylon and Perisphere were all it took to elevate these Eastman Kodak "Baby Brownie" and "Bullet" cameras to special-edition status. In the "Baby Brownie" (*left*), the Perisphere appears behind the shutter lever. In the "Bullet" model, the Trylon and Perisphere are applied above the lens.

The only things that made the World's Fair model of the Remington "Cadet" typewriter different from all other $20.95 "Cadet" portables were the application of a Trylon and Perisphere decal and a carrying case in the Fair's colors, orange and blue.

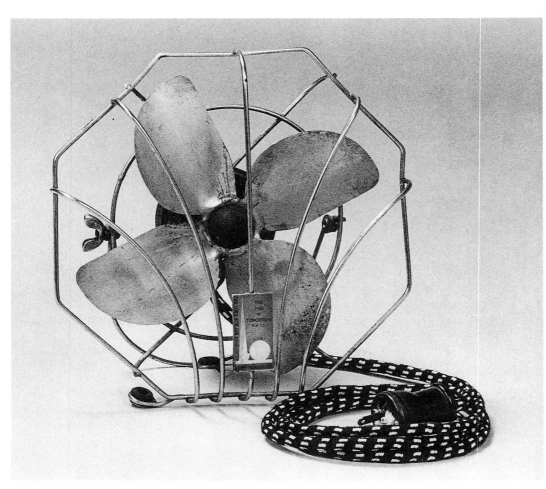

This electric fan, manufactured by the Knapp-Monarch Company of St. Louis, Missouri, bore a plate on the grille with a silhouette of the Trylon and Perisphere and the words, "THE FAN OF TOMORROW / K. M. Co."

One of many souvenir pocket watches sold at Fair concessions and in selected stores, this model, manufactured by the Ingersoll Clock Company, is shown with its original enameled case. When the case was folded face-down under the clock, it served as a watch stand. When the watch was in its case, the souvenir measured only 1⅝" high.

In the 1930s the Bissell carpet sweeper was so popular that its brand name, like that of Hershey's, was virtually a generic term. The company's slogan, "Every woman needs a Bissell," was known throughout the country—but universally snickered at in the outer boroughs of New York City, where the translation of the Yiddish phrase "a bissell" changed the meaning of the slogan to "Every woman needs a little." The special World's Fair edition of the carpet sweeper, known as "Bissell's Thirty Nine," featured the ubiquitous Trylon and Perisphere.

RCA Victor manufactured a special World's Fair table radio that pictured the outines of several exhibition buildings on the thermosetting plastic of the case. Featured prominently, of course, were the Trylon and Perisphere in white, near the speaker, and the RCA Building, to the right of the dial.

One of the more interesting aspects of collecting world's fair souvenirs is in observing how the Trylon and Perisphere are incorporated into the design of an object—functionally, inventively, or haphazardly. In the two pocket watches illustrated here, the Trylon and Perisphere form the hands of the Theme Time watch on the left, while the Perisphere provides the face for the second hand of the Ingraham watch on the right. "Theme Time" was the name given its Theme Center watches by the New Haven Clock Co. On the reverse side of the aluminum case is embossed: "NEW YORK WORLD'S FAIR 1939." The chrome-plated brass Ingraham timepiece spelled out "WORLDS FA(I)R NY" instead of using numerals on the face. In 1939, the nonjeweled watch retailed for $1.50, complete with fob.

Many world's fair commemorative plates and porcelains celebrated New York City, site not only of the Fair but of the inauguration of the first American president. The Staffordshire serving dish at the *right* pictures a view of the East River, looking south beneath the Williamsburg, Manhattan, and Brooklyn bridges to New York Bay and the Statue of Liberty. Marked on the back is "CROWN STAFFORDSHIRE/MADE IN ENGLAND." Also inscribed is a long statement to the effect that the plate was made exclusively for Davis Collamore & Co., Ltd., New York.

Colorful to the eye, but cheap to the touch are the inexpensive porcelain souvenirs *below*. Usually showing scenes that bear little resemblance to the actual setting, these Japanese pieces came in many shapes and sizes, usually marked either "JAPAN" or "MADE IN JAPAN."

The glazed pottery steins, marking time spent at Heineken's on the Zuider Zee, are stamped "1 L" on the back to indicate the one liter content. The name of the popular restaurant was changed to Heineken's Holland House in 1940.

Inexpensive glass tumblers were frequently sold in sets of six as advertising premiums by such newspapers as the New York *Journal-American* and were made by several glass manufacturing companies, among them Libby and Anchor Hocking.

Frequently a building commemorated on a plate didn't materialize in 1939 in quite the same way it was envisioned when the souvenir was designed in 1937 or 1938. The set of six commemorative plates pictured here is a case in point. Produced in England by Copeland for Abraham & Straus, they puportedly showed the Shelter Building, Food Building, Hall of Production, Textile Building, Hall of Communications, and the Marine Transportation Building. By 1939, three of the structures—Shelter, Production, and Textile—no longer went by their earlier names.

Usually found in blue (sometimes in black) with gold decoration, this sturdy china teapot is marked on the bottom: "A GENUINE/HALL CHINA/TEA POT/ MADE IN U.S.A./SOLD EXCLUSIVELY/ AT/NEW YORK WORLD'S FAIR/ 1939 [or 1940]."

Although artfully arranged to suggest a table setting for a world's fair dinner, these household souvenirs were never intended to be used *en suite*. The rare set of world's fair silverware by Tiffany & Co. includes a salad fork, dinner fork, knife, iced tea spoon, soup spoon, teaspoon, butter knife, and serving spoon. The Tiffany commemorative plate was intended for display in the china closet and not for use on the dining table. (It is described on page 204.) The Trylon and Perisphere paper napkin was not meant to touch the lips of those who dined *a la* Tiffany. The glass ashtray is one of hundreds of such inexpensive souvenirs produced by dozens of glass manufacturers.

Of the bowl and two plates pictured here, the bowl and the plate on the left are decorated with the same cubist-deco design, even though they were produced by two different manufacturers. The bowl is marked on the bottom: "UNION MADE/1939 NEW YORK WORLD'S FAIR/SOUVENIR—MADE BY/THE PADEN CITY POTTERY/MADE IN THE U.S.A./PADEN CITY, W. VA." The plate, made for the 1940 Fair, is marked on the back: "THE CROWN CHINA CO./MINERVA CO./[union label] /NATIONAL BROTHERHOOD/OPERATIVE POTTERS." The other commemorative plate, made in England, is marked on the back: "NEW YORK WORLD'S FAIR/1789-1939/J. & G. MEAKIN. / ENGLAND / LICENSE No. 1661."

These Homer Laughlin commemorative plates, designed by Charles Murphy, are among the most aesthetically pleasing of all New York World's Fair collectibles. Among the exhibition halls readily identifiable on the subtly colored border design are the Marine Transportation Building, the United States (Federal) Building, and the Communicaitons Building. The back of the 1939 plate is marked: "DECORATION BY CHARLES MURPHY/150th ANNIVERSARY / INAUGURATION / OF / GEORGE WASHINGTON/AS/FIRST PRESIDENT/OF THE UNITED STATES/1789-1939." The mark on the 1940 plate is identical, except that the dates are omitted.

The Lenox Company of Trenton, New Jersey, manufactured several porcelain souvenirs for the Fair, including vases, candy or cigarette dishes, and salt and pepper shakers, each available in white, dark blue, and pastel shades of yellow, pink, and green. (The Trylon and Perisphere would appear in white on these colored pieces.) The marks varied considerably, but would usually include the Lenox trademark and the words "LENOX/MADE IN U.S.A." Some pieces are marked for the store selling the china, for example: "DESIGNED IN HONOR OF/NEW YORK WORLD'S FAIR /OVINGTON'S/NEW YORK."

This set of graduated teapots, with matching cream pitcher and sugar bowl, includes an additional teapot (not shown) and an aluminum coffee filter insert. The teapots are marked on the bottom: "Porcelier [in script] /TRADE MARK/VITREOUS HAND DEC./CHINA /MADE IN U.S.A." The pitcher and bowl are unmarked.

Souvenir pottery and porcelain catered to differing tastes and ranged in quality from the ridiculous to the sublime. On this page are illustrated examples of both extremes. At the *right* are pieces of imitation Wedgwood Jasperware made by the Japanese for the five-and-dime market. The Japanese pitcher and tumbler set *below*, made of inexpensive stoneware in a mottled orange-brown color with blue decoration, was for the same market. Both wares are simply marked "JAPAN."

The commemorative plates sold by Tiffany & Co. were available in blue or reddish pink and were marked on the back in the same color as the plate: "MADE/ESPECIALLY FOR/TIFFANY & CO./NEW YORK WORLD'S FAIR/1939/ [trademark] ADAMS/EST 1657/ENGLAND/LICENSE 1661". In a circle enclosing this information were the words "MODERN NEW YORK • OLD NEW YORK •

TRANSPORTATION • CITY HALL • BRIDGE • LIBERTY • TUNNELS • CONSTRUCTION • TRANSPORTATION", perhaps a reference to the design of the plates' border.

In 1939 the Great Atlantic and Pacific Tea Co. chain of nationwide grocery stores packaged its house brand of vinegar in bottles embossed with a map of the world and the words, "WORLD'S FAIR 1939." The A&P wasn't hedging any bets. By not mentioning either New York or San Francisco by name, it could use the same bottle on both coasts. In the same photograph is a glazed souvenir plate, and its original box, from the American Potter exhibit in the Home Furnishings Building. The plate is marked on the back: "JOINT EXHIBIT OF CAPTIAL AND LABOR/THE AMERICAN POTTER/NEW YORK/WORLD'S FAIR/ 1939."

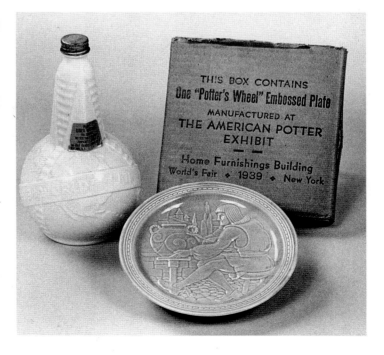

Opposite page: At the American Potter exhibit, George and Martha Washington ornaments were sold. The marks on these pieces vary, but usually include the words "THE AMERICAN POTTER/NEW YORK WORLD'S FAIR 1939 [or 1940]"

Also sold at the American Potter exhibit was a handsome art deco platter. It carries the same Charles Murphy design as the Homer Laughlin plates

on page 203 and was made by the Edwin M. Knowles China Co.

Illustrated together are additional examples of commemorative plates: The plate at the upper left is marked, "SARREGUEMINES, France." The Japanese plate to the right is similar to the wares shown on page 200. The plate commemorating the royal visit to the Fair is marked "ROYAL MINTON/GRIMWATER/ENGLAND."

Several manufacturers produced fabrics using design motifs borrowed from the Fair. Some fabrics used repeats of the Trylon and Perisphere, others incorporated several pavilions into the design. The unidentified maker of the fabric used to make this shirt adapted the Staehle poster shown on page 219 for the design. Shown next to the shirt is one of the better-designed pieces of jewelry made to celebrate the Fair, a gold pin with a blue enamel ground for a gold Trylon and Perisphere.

Compacts, fancy cases for carrying face powder, complete with powder puff and small mirror (usually affixed to the inside lid), were *de rigueur* until fairly recently. No woman could be considered properly dressed without one in her purse or evening bag. From at least early in the century, compacts of every shape, form, and material were manufactured as souvenirs for fairs, and the New York World's Fair was no exception. The compacts shown on the *opposite page* are just a small sample of the large number produced. Most are enameled metal, some with, applied plastic decoration; still others, applied metal decoration to leather cases or needlepoint applied to metal. Makers' names found frequently within such compacts include Girex and Zell (on powder puffs) and Gwenda ("made in England") and Zell ("made in U.S.A.").

"During the visit to the fair of King George VI and Queen Elizabeth in June 1939, " writes Helen Harrison, "the Queen reportedly remarked that she was sorry that her children, the Princesses Elizabeth and Margaret, had not shared the experience with her. As a gesture or good will, a large selection of souvenirs was dispatched to Buckingham Palace for the enjoyment and education of the future Queen Elizabeth II, her sister, and their friends." By far the most special gift for the royal princesses was the framed collection of enameled plated brass state flowers shown above. The gift was inscribed, "TO/ELIZABETH AND MARGARET ROSE OF ENGLAND/AND ALL THE CHILDREN OF THE BRITISH EMPIRE/FROM THE YOUTH OF AMERICAN DEMOCRACY."

Although many of the necklaces, charm bracelets, pins, rings, tie clips, and cuff links and other pieces of inexpensive jewelry made for the Fair have an undeniably nostalgic charm, they were intended as souvenirs and not for serious wear. Their quality was of the sort that turns the skin green on touch.

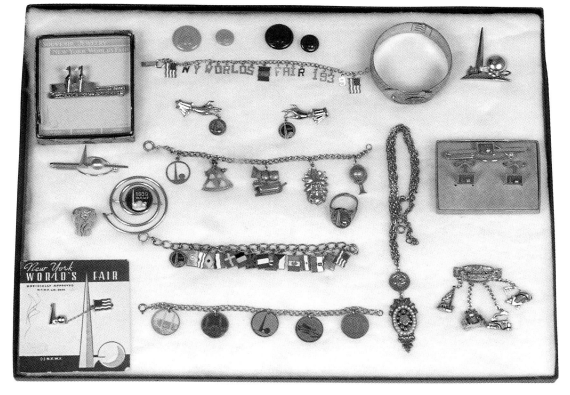

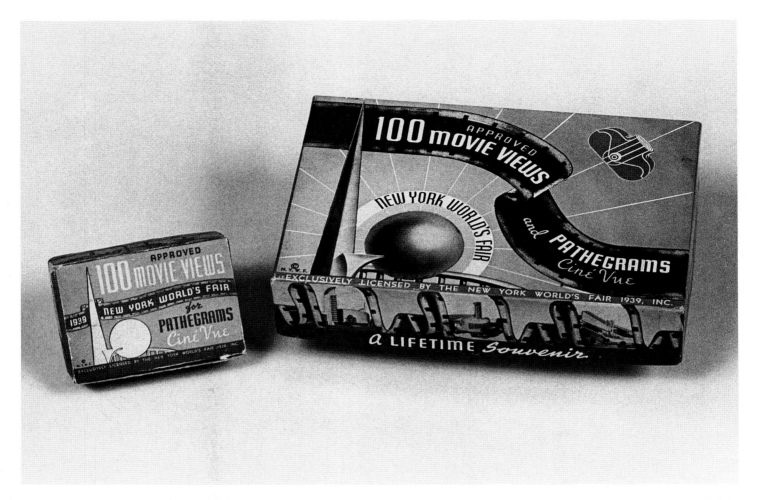

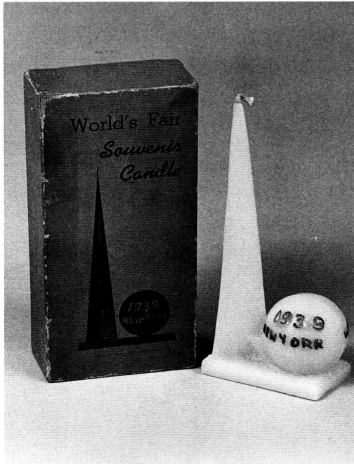

When a loop of film was loaded into a "Cine Vue" hand viewer and held to the light, scenes of the Fair could be seen by looking into the eye piece and then turning the knob to see the next scene. The plastic viewer was manufactured by Pathegrams, Inc., New York City.

Among the many souvenirs made in the image of the Trylon and Perisphere was this candle, manufacturer unidentified.

This unmarked leather handkerchief box contained several machine-embroidered cotton handkerchiefs, such as the one shown.

Medallions are particularly treasured souvenirs of the New York World's Fair. The gold-plated brass example shown pictures both the Theme Center and Washington.

From 1938 through 1940, New York State advertised the Fair on vehicular license plates. The 1938 and 1940 plates had yellow numerals against a black background; the 1939 plates, the reverse.

Among leather souvenirs were, *clockwise from top,* autograph albums (made by M. Picot, Brooklyn New York), diaries to record one's visit to the Fair (made by Pocasset Press, New York), ladies' "necessaries" (including mirror and plastic comb), and five-year diaries (made in Japan).

Perfumes made for the Fair were to Chanel No. 5 what Fair jewelry was to Tiffany. Illustrated here are Rubicon Parfum's "Trylon"; enameled containers of three half-ounce bottles of "Sweet Pea," "Gardenia," and "Lilac," by Duvinne, New York; and "Perfume Caravan by Karoff," manufactured by Stuart Products Co., St. Paul, Minnesota.

A relatively rare collector's find is this white metal replica of the statue of the Russian worker that appeared atop the Soviet Pavilion. The statuette measures 9¾″ from base to star.

Equally unusual is this set of machine-knit cotton golf-club covers, manufacturer unidentified. Among the color combinations were green and black, orange and blue, and orange and black.

Far more common souvenirs were pocket knives, most with plastic or mother-of-pearl shafts marked with the words, "New York World's Fair 1939." Among the more unusual knives were a fish knife marked "Colonial Prov. R.I." on the serrated blade (*top, center*), and, shown beneath it, a "souvenir coin-knife," a perfectly useless novelty that combined two unlike objects to no particular effect. Like the coin-knife, most of the knives shown here were made by Colonial. The black knife to the right of the coin-knife is marked "Hammer Brand."

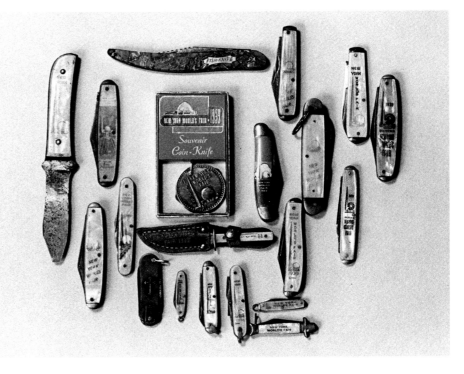

Gifts for smokers are common world's fair souvenirs. In the photograph *above* are seen, *clockwise from top*, a gift pack of Lucky Strike cigarettes, mailable from the American Tobacco Company Building for fourteen cents; a yellow metal cigarette case, marked inside "ELGIN AMERICAN/MADE IN U.S.A."; two white metal "Letter Case" cigarette cases, marked inside "Harry N. Richman Co./Made in U.S.A.", one with the recipient's name inscribed in ink and varnished; an enameled Bakelite cigarette box, maker unidentified; two Bakelite and chrome-plated "Silent Flame" table lighters by Dunhill; and an enameled cigarette case, marked inside "GWENDA/MADE IN ENGLAND."

Seen to the *left* are a china Trylon and Perisphere combination cigarette box and ashtray, marked on the bottom "H/ Japan" (the lid of the Perisphere cigarette box is removable); an original box of a Firestone rubber tire ashtray; a rubber tire ashtray from the B. F. Goodrich Company, marked "GOODRICH SILVERTOWN 6.00-10 4 PLY GOLDEN PL 4" on tire; and a blue enamel "three-ring" ashtray, made for the Ballantine Inn by Scammell's Lamberton China, Trenton, New Jersey.

Several briar pipes in the shape of the Trylon and Perisphere were made for smokers. The pipe shown has a small Trylon and Perisphere impressed on the stem; other pipes had "NEW YORK WORLD'S FAIR 1939" in raised letters on the bowl.

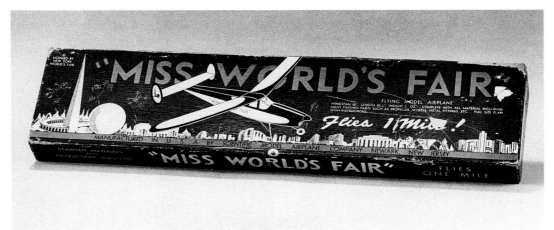

Many toys and games for children were made under license to the New York World's Fair Corporation, several of which are illustrated on the pages following.

Bobby and Betty were two fictitious (and "golly, gee whiz-type") children who were the subject of a promotional film about the fair and of a children's book based on that film. They were also at the center of a 1939 board game, "Bobby and Betty's Trip to the New York World's Fair" (*above*), made by Parker Brothers, Inc., distributors of "Monopoly," introduced only four years earlier. The bird's-eye view of the Fair used on the board is by John Wenrich and was first published in the April 1938 issue of the *New York World's Fair Bulletin*.

"Miss World's Fair," a model airplane ("Flies 1 Mile!"), was manufactured by Scientific Model Airplane Company, Newark, New Jersey, and was packaged with all needed parts and instructions for assembly.

Dolls dressed in the native garb of foreign lands had been popular in America since at least the end of the nineteenth century, so it was only logical that dolls representing nationals of foreign pavilions should be sold at the Fair. Dutch dolls, for example, were manufactured by N. W. Bouwes of Edam by license from the Fair Corporation. The peasant doll illustrated at the *right*, with a celluloid head on a cloth body, more than likely represented Poland, or possibly Czechoslovakia. The doll representing a Fair guide also has a celluloid head and a cloth body. Embossed on the back of its hat is "©NYWF". The drum by which the dolls stand is actually an orange and blue cardboard candy box, but the maker of the sweets is unidentified.

It was only a matter of time before the Trylon and Perisphere suggested themselves to some perfervid imagination as a gigantic ring toss in the sky, and, sure enough, a Trylon and Perisphere ring toss game (*below*) was manufactured by L. Pressman & Co., Inc., of New York City.

By peeping through the hole in this cardboard peepshow, the viewer was able to see an imaginary vista of Constitution Mall and the Trylon and Perisphere in three dimensions. The peepshow is marked, "The World of Tomorrow/New York World's Fair/ Copyright by Elizabeth Sage Hare and Warren Chappell." Little is known about the manufacture of this peepshow, but the prevailing myth among collectors is that it was produced in Germany, and that the outbreak of war limited the number shipped to America.

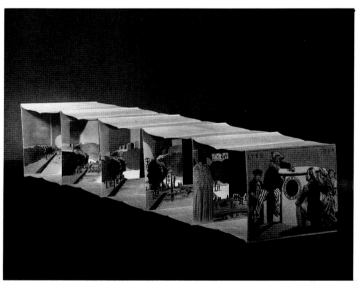

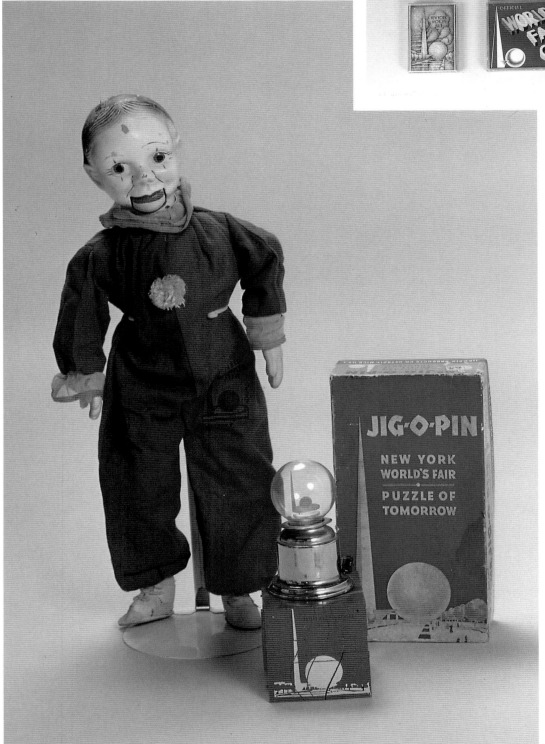

Many makers of playing cards were licensed to manufacture cards featuring a view of the Fair on each card. Cards were available in single or double deck packages. Among the makers of the cards *above* were the United States Playing Card Co., Cincinnati, Ohio, and Congress Playing Cards. Also shown *above* is the "Official World's Fair Game," a card game using illustrations of buildings at the Fair, produced by Parker Brothers, Inc.

The doll at the *left* is believed to be Edgar Bergen's dummy, Charlie McCarthy, dressed as a clown and may have been associated with the Chase & Sanborn exhibit in the Standard Brands Building. Chase & Sanborn Coffee was the sponsor of Bergen's popular radio program.

"Jig-O-Pin," a game billed as the "Puzzle of Tomorrow," consisted of sixty-four jigsaw-cut pieces that, when correctly assembled, fit on four pins to form a cube. The six sides of the cube pictured five Fair buildings, including the Trylon and Perisphere, and Mr. Jig-O-Pin. The game was manufactured by Jig-O-Pin Products Co., Detroit, Michigan.

The assembled Jig-O-Pin cube is supporting a true collector's prize, a lamp with a Trylon and Perisphere-filament bulb. (When lit, the filament glows blue-red.) The bulb was manufactured by Aerolux, which in 1939 was located at 653 Eleventh Avenue, New York.

Several companies manufactured models of World's Fair buildings to be self-assembled. Among them was Standard Toycraft Products of New York, whose "Build-Your-Own New York World's Fair" is illustrated at the *right*.

Shown *below* is an assembled variation on the "build-your-own" theme, an assemble-it-yourself model that is also a board game. The box in which the model/game was packaged suggests the game that was to be played after the cutouts were assembled: "MINIA-TURE NEW YORK WORLD'S FAIR 1939/BUILD UP TOY/ CARDBOARD CUT OUTS AND PINKIE /GAME OF LUCK AND SKILL/RACE THROUGH/ THE FAIR GROUNDS/ BUILDUP TOYS, INC., NYC."

No one knows for certain how many souvenirs were made in the shape of the Trylon and Perisphere, but there were certainly several hundred. Shown on this page are a representative sample.

There were thermometers made from the Theme Center and banks, too, but the metal object at the *left* may well be the only combination thermometer/bank that incorporates the Trylon and Perisphere. Its maker is unidentified, but the piece itself was acquired from the collection of Edwin H. Mosler, Jr., New York City, whose Mosler Safe Company exhibited at the Fair.

Among the Trylon and Perisphere souvenirs illustrated *above* are, from left to right, an orange and white china salt and pepper shaker set (marked "H/JAPAN" on bottom of stand); a cast-iron doorstop (maker unidentified); a Bakelite thermometer (maker unidentified); an inexpensive china knicknack (mark obscured); a pair of painted wooden bookends (original price label of twenty-nine cents affixed to base); a nickel-plated white metal inkwell (stamped on bottom, "MADE IN FRANCE"); a battery-operated lamp (maker unidentified); and a marble bookend, imported from Italy (maker unidentified).

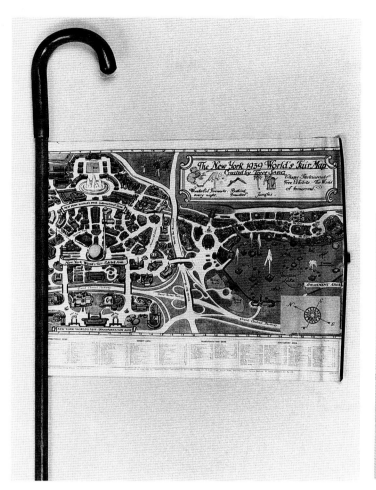

Getting around the Fair was not always easy on the feet, and various walkers' aids were offered for sale. Although there were souvenir canes (*left*) of every variety and size, the most unusual cane of all was certainly the one that provided a fold-out copy of Tony Sarg's famous map of the Fair (*above*). The unique device was produced by the In-A-Cane Display Company of Boston, Massachusetts. Sarg, a popular artist of the thirties, had his own exhibit at the Fair. The cover of his well-known map is shown *above*. Fairgoers needed ample muscle to lug these combination cane/seats (*right*) with them. Made of solid wood, they were anything but lightweight. Decorated with a Fair decal on the seat, the "Kan-O-Seats" are marked on the bottom of the seat, "KAN-O-SEAT/PAT MAY 21 1935/STAFFORD-JOHNSON CORP./IONA/MICH." A similar device, called a "Swagger Seat," was manufactured by the Swagger Seat Corporation of Hudson Falls, New York.

Evocative posters, representing the best of late-thirties graphic design, were created to advertise the 1939 Fair. Among the best are those illustrated on these pages: Albert Staehle's poster of a "girl guide" waving potential fairgoers into the Fair; an unidentified artist's poster inviting Dutch tourists to sail to the Fair via the Holland-America Line; Leslie Ragan's poster urging visitors to use America's railroads to attend both the New York and San Francisco fairs; and John Atherton's poster of "Mithrana," an allegorical representation of the Fair. On the *opposite page* is Joseph Binder's visual epitomization of the Trylon and Perisphere. This famous poster won first prize in the New York World's Fair poster competition of 1938.

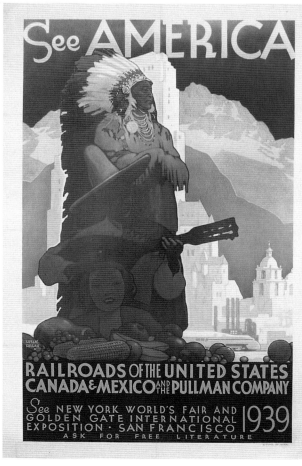

NEW YORK WORLD'S FAIR
THE WORLD OF TOMORROW 1939

Four months after the fair that hailed the World of Tomorrow opened, Germany invaded Poland. When the Fair reopened for the 1940 season, the tone of the event had changed. Gone was any talk of international interdependence. The new slogan, "For Peace and Freedom," played down internationalism and emphasized all things American. Posters that a year earlier had been futuristic were now folksy and featured a rosy-cheeked, middle-aged middle-American named Elmer. "Makes you proud to be an American," he proclaimed of the Fair. Hitler had successfully changed the World of Tomorrow into a super county fair. Shown on these pages are typical posters of the 1940 season, advertisements that reflect a reduced admission charge, from the seventy-five cents of 1939 to the fifty of 1940.

FOR
PEACE
AND
FREEDOM

World's Fair OF 1940
★★ NEW YORK ★★

ADMISSION 50¢   OPENS MAY 11ᵀᴴ

Popular songs have always been associated with world's fairs, with one fair, the St. Louis Exposition of 1904, having even produced a nationwide song hit, "Meet Me in St. Louis, Louie." Although many songs grew out of the New York World's Fair—from the event itself and from its various stage shows—no hits were forthcoming. In fact, most of the music is now justly forgotten, preserved in sheet music and on rare 78-rpm records.

"Dawn of a New Day," written by George and Ira Gershwin, and published in 1938, is perhaps the best-known song to have grown out of the Fair. In a preface to its sheet music (*opposite page*), the story of its genesis is told: "The music for this song was found among the papers of the late George Gershwin . . . Before his death in 1937, he had hoped to compose some music for the New York World's Fair of 1939. The discovery of this song, 'Dawn of a New Day,' seems to indicate that the mood and rhythm of 'The World of Tomorrow' had long been on his mind. Ira Gershwin, who wrote the lyrics that helped make the Gershwin songs famous, has composed the lyrics of this song especially for the Fair. The verses express the basic idea of the whole enterprise." Although the song was recorded and heavily promoted, it never took off. The music,

unfortunately, was second-drawer George; the lyrics, third-drawer Ira.

In 1940, "Dawn of a New Day" was replaced as the "official song of the New York World's Fair" by Eugene La Barre's "For Peace and Freedom" (not shown). It was monumentally awful and mercifully forgotten.

DAWN OF A NEW DAY

by
GEORGE GERSHWIN
and IRA GERSHWIN

SONG OF THE NEW YORK WORLD'S FAIR
1939

CHAPPELL
& CO·INC·
RKO BUILDING
ROCKEFELLER
CENTER·N·Y·C
CHAPPELL
MADE IN U·S·A· & CO·LTD·LONDON

Together, the Trylon and Perisphere was such a potent symbol that it appeared on uncountable magazine covers, books, and other printed matter. The three examples on this page are joined by others on the pages following. Shown here are the memorable cover of a special World's Fair issue of the French magazine, *L'Illustration,* Leo Rackow's witty cover for the May 1939 issue of *Modern Packaging*, and the Manhattan classified telephone directory for spring-summer 1939.

There were literally thousands of souvenir books and brochures published for the Fair, each of them different from the other. Booklets were printed for free distribution at individual pavilions, booths, and displays. Other booklets were printed as programs of special events and were sold for a nominal fee. Still others were published as official souvenir "views" of the Fair, to be taken home and cherished. Shown here is a fraction of a fraction of the paper ephemera engendered by the Fair. Included are the official guide books of the 1939 and 1940 seasons, a typical book of views, and a coloring book for children.

Throughout 1939 and 1940, the New York World's Fair made its way to the cover of virtually every magazine in the nation. In 1939 alone, the *New Yorker* featured the Fair on no fewer than seven issues of the magazine. The magazine covers shown on these pages, while a representative sample, hardly do justice to the great variety of graphic treatments given the Fair by some of the best commercial artists of the period.

One cover shown will evidently surprise many readers, since it is hardly general knowledge that Batman, Robin, and Superman attended the Fair in 1940. If one is to take their many adventures in *World's Fair Comics* seriously, then so many international criminals converged on the Fair that the super-heroes' crime-stopping services were much in demand. One wonders what Fiorello LaGuardia had to say about this.

15 CENTS

JUNE 24, 1939

The Billboard

SUMMER SPECIAL

NEW YORK WORLD'S FAIR .. THE WORLD OF TOMORROW

1939

Another source of delight to collectors are the many menus from World's Fair restaurants. Not only are these collectibles of interest for their handsome graphics, but they are suggestive of both culinary tastes and their cost in 1939-40. The menus illustrated here offer a representative range of restaurants and prices, from the least to the most expensive. Examples: fairgoers could get a plate of spaghetti at Caruso for fifty cents, or a Long Island duckling dinner at the YMCA restaurant for a dollar. A lobster dinner at Schaefer Center was a dollar and a half, while a filet mignon at Rondevoo was fifteen cents less. Prime ribs at the expensive Three Crowns cost two and a half dollars, while dinner at the famous restaurant in the French Pavilion (*opposite page*) was not half as dear as one would have expected it to be—even in 1939 dollars.

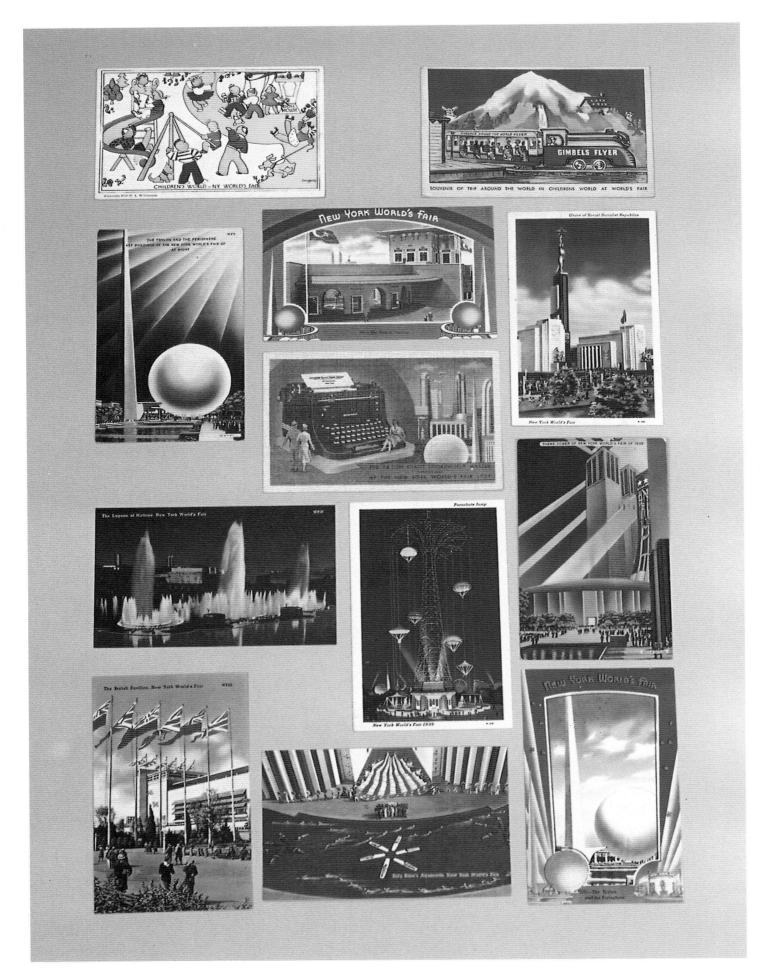

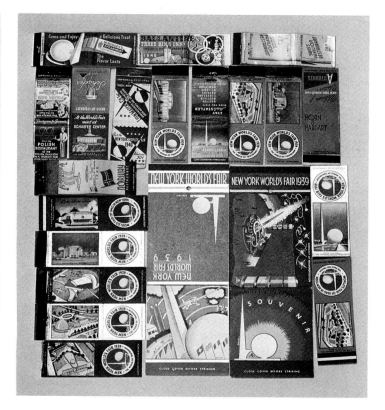

As in any other area of collecting, memorabilia of the New York World's Fair are so extensive that specialized subjects have emerged for concentrated study. For example, so many postcards were issued for the Fair—close to a thousand, at least—that collecting them all might be the quest of a lifetime. Among the cards shown on the *opposite page*, the rarest is unquestionably the second from the bottom on the right—a 1936 rendering of the proposed Theme Center, before the design of the Trylon and Perisphere was officially adopted. Among the many makers who published postcards for the Fair were the Exposition Souvenir Corp., C. T. Art-Colortone, Tichnor Quality Views, Manhattan Post Card Publishing Co., and the Albertype Co.

Other specialized areas of World's Fair collecting include tickets and passes to events (*above, left*), matchbooks (*above, right*), and silkscreened pennants and banners. Banners and velvet flags of the Fair were particularly colorful. The example to the left is made of silk.

In order to process the volume of mail both to and from the Fair, a special World's Fair branch of the United States Post Office was established on Main Street, just west of the Communications Building, and collection boxes were located throughout the grounds. Fifty years later, a concrete reminder of the Fair's post office branch become apparent each time a collector locates a postcard or letter mailed from the World of Tomorrow. The cancellation mark "WORLD'S FAIR STA." lends a much greater nostalgic value to a postcard than one from Jersey City—and, sometimes, if on a World's Fair commemorative stamp, a slight monetary value as well.

There are several types of postage stamps of interest to collectors of World's Fair memorabilia. Particularly collectible are the commemorative stamps issued in the United States and in many foreign countries to honor the Fair. Even more prized are first day issues of these stamps. And even rarer are first day issues mailed to people associated with the Fair. (A related category of collecting is the preservation of correspondence to and from administrators, architects, designers, artists, and other Fair personnel.)

Illustrated on the *opposite page* are a first day issue of the official United States World's Fair stamp, a three-cent stamp with a white Trylon and Perisphere against a deep-blue ground; a letter from Moscow, bearing two different stamps commemorating the Soviet Pavilion; and a 1940 letter to the Overseas Trade Department of the British Pavilion with a stamp honoring the establishment of penny postage in 1840.

Shown on this page, *clockwise from top left,* are a Mexican air-mail stamp commemorating the Mexican Building in the Hall of Nations; a first day issue of a stamp honoring the seventy-fifth anniversary of the Thirteenth Amendment to the Constitution, and cancelled at the World's Fair Post Office; a closeup of the British stamp shown on the previous page; a French stamp, juxtaposing the French Pavilion and the Statue of Liberty to commemorate the Fair; and a close-up of the official United States World's Fair stamp.

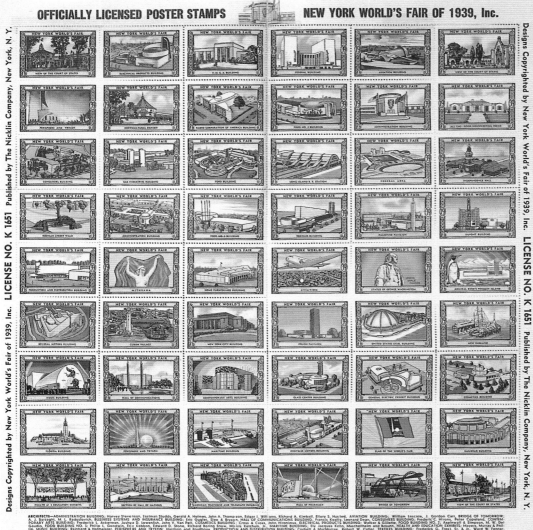

Opposite page: One of the many patches given Fair personnel for their uniforms or work clothes is shown next to two of the most popular souvenirs distributed at the Fair—a Bakelite pin, made, of course, of Bakelite and given those who watched their manufacture in several colors within the Hall of Industrial Science, and the Heinz pickle pin, a staple of world's fair giveaways since 1893.

An assortment of souvenir decals and pinbacks, shown side by side, represents only a fraction of the many colorful stickers and pins that Fairgoers gathered with avidity. Given away by New York hotels and World's Fair exhibitors, decals were used on luggage or preserved in scrapbooks. Pins served several purposes, among them identification of guests at special events and as inexpensive advertising premiums for consumers. Both are as eagerly collected today as they were in 1939-40.

This page: Official poster stamps of the New York World's Fair were manufactured and distributed by the Nicklin Company of New York City. The set was described in advertisements as consisting of "54 different scenes—all in color. One set, 15¢; 2 sets, 25¢; 5 sets, 50¢; 10 sets, $1.10." (Those who had fingers to count with obviously bought two sets of five before buying a set of ten.) A legend at the bottom of each set identifies the architects and sculptors of the buildings and sculptures illustrated.

Among the most common, but most prized, souvenirs of the Fair are the "I Have Seen the Future" pin, given visitors to General Motors' Futurama, and the Mr. Peanut pin, given those who witnessed "The Adventures of Mr. Peanut in Tiny Town" at the Planters Nut & Chocolate Co. display in the Food Building.

Afterword

On October 18, 1940, the Bronx Home News, a New York City newspaper, ran the following editorial:

Time is fleeting, and any New Yorker who fails to make a visit to the World's Fair before the end of next week will forego the final opportunity to behold the wonders of an international exposition the equal of which probably will not be seen again in this generation, if ever.

This realization has begun to seep into the minds of multitudes within the city and of throngs from without, as evidenced by the record-breaking crowds that swarmed over the 1,200 acres in Flushing Meadows during the past two weekends.

Sunday, October 27th, will be the closing day. It will be like the end of a world—a world of dazzling exhibits and displays, of charm, glamor and gayety. The imaginative "World of Tomorrow" will be no more. The 25,000,000 persons who paid their way through its gates last year, the 18,000,000 or so who will have entered as paying customers before this season ends, will then be confronted solely with the actual world of tomorrow, which from all indications will be a harsh and comfortless contrast to Grover Whalen's paradise.

The Trylon and Perisphere will come down, and the city's skyline will be much poorer for the loss.

Democracity, now housed within the Perisphere, will disappear, and with it will go its idealistic vision of happy men and women living in amity in a miraculous city of the future. The General Motors Futurama will be dismantled. Man-made thunder will cease to peal and man-made lightning to flash within General Electric's Steinmetz Auditorium. There will be no nightly extravaganza of fountains, flames, and fireworks over the Lagoon of Nations, and the millions of eyes that have been bewildered and enchanted by this spectacle will look elsewhere in vain for comparable entertainment.

An evil fate has pursued the Fair. When it opened in the spring of 1939, as an unprecedented $155,000,000 exhibition of man's accomplishments on this earth, dedicated to freedom and democracy and brotherhood, it was hailed universally. No great nation was unrepresented, save one—Germany. But the Fair's mission of world peace was set at naught by the coming of war, and its international section was decimated and its Court of Peace made a travesty by the hand of Mars.

The Fair in its first year did compile a greater attendance than ever did any other World's Fair, yet the number was far below expectations. Reduction in admission charges, bargain features, contests and prizes, informalization—all have failed to keep this season's attendance even at last year's levels. Long stretches of bad weather, the disruption of the international area, the fatal attraction of the war news which keeps people's minds so occupied that they look less for other "amusements"—have taken their toll at the expense of the Fair.

This week the Fair plays host, without charge, to 250,000 adults on the city's relief rolls. This is a fine gesture for the closing days. There are millions of other adults and children who should attend. New York had its last World's Fair in 1853—eighty-seven years ago. The next one may come before the year 2027, but it is a safe bet that it will not come in the lifetime of most of us.

The New York World's Fair closed on October 27, 1940.

America entered the war a little more than a year later.

New York held another World's Fair in 1964-65, within the lifetime of many who had attended the 1939 Fair.

It did not hold a candle to The World of Tomorrow, the equal of which will not be seen again.

Credits and Bibliography

CREDITS

Many of the photographs in this book were originally used to publicize the Fair by the New York World's Fair Corporation, an organization long ago dissolved. Every effort has been made to locate copyright holders of these publicity photos, and any inadvertent oversights will be corrected in subsequent editions.

The photographs by Melville David Weingarten included herein are reproduced from the collection of, and with the permission of, Catherine Yronwode.

Many surviving color photographs of the Fair have faded to an unattractive ghostly pink. Happily, the color photographs taken by Conrad H. Ruppert in 1939-40 have survived with their original rainbow hues still true. Photographs from Mr. Ruppert's collection are reproduced with his permission.

Most of the World's Fair souvenirs included in chapter 13 were photographed by Ken White and are from the collection of Herbert Rolfes.

The World of Tomorrow could not have been completed without the generous assistance and encouragement of John M. Anton, Bruce H. Baker, Beverly Ball Chassler, John Danko, Eamon Dolan, Lawrence Grow, Ken Jennings, Addie Kaplan, Beth Kalet, Ronald R. Misiur, Betsy Rolfes, Ned Smith, and Fran Smythe.

BIBLIOGRAPHY

Appelbaum, Stanley. *The New York World's Fair 1939/ 1940 in 155 Photographs by Richard Wurts and Others.* New York: Dover Publications, 1977.

Bainbridge, John and St. Clair McKelway. "That Was the New York World's Fair." *The New Yorker* (April 19, 1941): 35-46.

Black, John. *Songs of the World's Fair.* Boston: Bruce Humphries, 1939.

Bliven, Bruce, Jr. "Fair Tomorrow." *The New Republic* 97 (December 7, 1938): 119-21.

_____. "Gone Tomorrow." *The New Republic* 99 (May 17, 1939): 40-42.

Duffus, R. L. "The Beginning of a World, Not the End." *The New York Times Magazine* (July 2, 1939): 1-2, 15.

Edwards, Catherine Conrad. "Take Them to the Fair." *Parents Magazine* 14 (April, 1939): 26-27.

Elsie-Jean. *A Trip to the World's Fair with Bobby and Betty.* New York: Dodge Publications, 1938.

Greif, Martin. *Depression Modern: The Thirties Style in America.* New York: Universe Books, 1975.

Gutheim, F. A. "Buildings at the Fair." *The Magazine of Art* 32 (May, 1939): 286-97.

Harding, Gardner L. "World's Fair, New York." *Harper's Magazine* 179 (July, 1939): 193-200.

Haskell, Douglas. "At the Fair." *The Nation* 148 (May 20, 1939): 594.

Lehman, Arnold L. *1930's Expositions.* Dallas: Dallas Museum of Fine Arts, 1972.

Lippman, Walter. "A Day at the World's Fair." *Current History* 50 (July, 1939): 50-51.

Marquis, Alice Goldfarb. *Hopes and Ashes: The Birth of Modern Times.* New York: The Free Press, 1986.

Meikle, Jeffrey L. *Twentieth Century Limited: Industrial Design in America, 1925-1939.* Philadelphia: Temple University Press, 1979.

Harrison, Helen A., ed. *Dawn of a New Day.* New York: Queens Museum and New York University Press, 1980.

Monaghan, Frank, ed. *Official Souvenir Book, New York World's Fair 1939.* New York: Exposition Publications, 1939.

Moses, Robert. "From Dump to Glory: Corona Dumps." *Saturday Evening Post* 210 (January 15, 1938): 12-13.

Mullen, Robert R. and Walter S. Jordan. "A Day in the World of Tomorrow." *Christian Science Monitor* (June 10, 1939): 8-9.

"The New York Fair." *Architectural Forum* (June, 1939): 395-462.

New York World's Fair Licensed Merchandise. New York: New York World's Fair Merchandising Department, 1939.

Pringle, Henry Fowles. "Stupendous, Colossal, Terrific." *Ladies Home Journal* 56 (June, 1939): 14-15.

Shalett, Sidney M. "Epitaph for the World's Fair." *Harper's Magazine* 182 (December, 1940): 22-31.

"Symphonies in Sight and Sound Designed by J. Labatut." *The Magazine of Art* 32 (May, 1939): 290.

"Take the Fair Home." *House Beautiful* 81 (June, 1939): 30-31.

"Trends of Tomorrow: Report on What the New York World's Fair Means to Decoration." *House and Garden* 76 (July, 1939): 14-35.

Index